An Existentialist Curriculum of Action

Creating a Language of Freedom and Possibility

Shaireen Rasheed

UNIVERSITY PRESS OF AMERICA,® INC.

Lanham • Boulder • New York • Toronto • Plymouth, UK

Copyright © 2007 by
University Press of America,® Inc.
4501 Forbes Boulevard
Suite 200
Lanham, Maryland 20706
UPA Acquisitions Department (301) 459-3366

Estover Road
Plymouth PL6 7P
United Kingdom

Library of Congress Control Number: 2006933793
ISBN-13: 978-0-7618-3591-2 (paperback : alk. paper)
ISBN-10: 0-7618-3591-1 (paperback : alk. paper)

$\otimes$™ The paper used in this publication meets the minimum
requirements of American National Standard for Information
Sciences—Permanence of Paper for Printed Library Materials,
ANSI Z39.48—1984

To Mariam—my muse

Contents

Acknowledgements

This book is the result of my dissertation six years ago at Columbia University under the guidance of Rene Arcilla, Nel Noddings and Maxine Greene and I am eternally grateful to them for this project. I have since reworked and revisited my manuscript to reflect its current form. I am also grateful to my colleagues and students at Long Island University who have supported me through my endeavor. I would also like to thank Linda ONeil for her constructive editorial feedback. On a personal note I would like to thank my parents for their constant love and encouragement; to my sisters for always being there for me. My greatest debt is to my husband and best friend Zahid for his patience and unending support and to my children Mariam and Mikail for being my oxygen. This book is a dedication to my mother and to all the women in my life whose struggles, experiences and triumphs have created a space for freedom and possibility to exist.

Chapter Two has been adapted from Shaireen Rasheed, "The Existential Concept of Freedom for Maxine Greene: The Influence of Sartre and Merleau-Ponty on Greene's Educational Pedagogy," in Philosophy of Education 2002, ed. Scott Fletcher (Urbana, Illinois: Philosophy of Education Society, 2003), 394-401. Reprinted by permission of Philosophy of Education Society.

A revised version of Chapter Five can be found at Rasheed S., "Naming and the Existentialist Curriculum of Action: Creating a Pluralistic Pedagogy." *International Journal of Pedagogies and Learning*, 1(2), October 2005, an open access journal whose articles are free to use, with proper attribution, in educational and other non-commercial settings. (http://www.usqu.edu.au/education/ijpl/default.htm)

Introduction: Language and the Curriculum of Action

One of the present movement toward educational reform, with its rationalistic and technologically oriented curricular objectives and overtones of a national curriculum, threatens to eliminate the broad citizenship function of schools in favor of a restrictive, market-and-workplace-skills perspective. This "mode of teaching," as Robert Connel says in his essay "Poverty and Education," "assumes that knowledge is an objectifiable, quantifiable thing"[1]

Enforcing the new curricular standards that have been legislated by the state on the initiative of state education agencies, according to some, heightens the problem of discipline; moreover, insofar as these standards are successfully enforced, they divide pupils into an "academically successful minority" and an "academically discredited majority".[2] By ignoring the fact that classrooms contain people as well as information, educators working within the formalistic paradigms have created a technocratic curriculum that, instead of promoting critical thinking, reinforces a repetitive, uncreative concept of education. As Theodore Sizer speculates: "Perhaps Americans don't want question askers, people who want answers. Perhaps in sum, the unchallenged mindlessness of so much of the status quo is truly acceptable; it doesn't make waves."[3]

A teacher within this framework who wants her students to know more is essentially concerned with giving the students more of what she, the expert, knows. Typical of this kind of education, then, is the teacher lecture. Textbooks provide information, and the teacher-expert clarifies or embellishes this information for students. Students merely listen and take notes. Testing is the characteristic form of assessment, and the test questions characteristically have only one right answer. The teacher stands alone as authority, the expert who dispenses knowledge.

Along with its effect on the relationship between teachers and students, the presence of meaningful curriculum that engages and motivates students emerges as a key to leveling the national playing field. Schools will continue, unless crucial curriculum issues are addressed, to separate "winners" from "losers"—despite the lip-service paid to equal opportunity. These issues include what is studied, how the curriculum is selected, and how the curriculum relates to the lives of the students. In other words, educators need to develop a definition of curriculum that establishes a theoretical basis for the program.

Moreover, the literature on school improvements suggests that teachers and school staff must achieve a shared sense of vision and purpose in which to ground their relationships with one another and with their students. Presently, by contrast, the absence of such a sense of connectedness afflicts much of our educational life. Schooling must cease to be seen solely as a means by which individuals can advance their own economic well-being. Instead the educational process must be redefined to enable students to find and develop their individual identities. Teacher training programs need to inspire their students to get involved, to make a difference, and to "lay bare the ways in which meaning is produced and mobilized for the maintenance of education"[4] Students in turn need to be given the chance to explore the infinite variety of ways in which the process of learning can take place.

If curriculum theory is to facilitate the expansion of a democratic curriculum and set of social relations, a theory of language must be employed that will expand the possible ways of writing, reading, speaking, listening, and hearing. As educators, we must develop a curriculum discourse that cultivates critical interchange regarding the quality and purpose of schooling and of human life. This will encourage perspectives that enrich rather than restrict the field of education. Such a project is implicit in the post-modern readings of educational politics carried out by Henry Giroux and others. As Giroux states:

> A language of educational theory needs to be created by educationalists that will make them reflective to the politics of their own lived situation. At best such a language would make administrators, teachers and other cultural workers self conscious of the historically contingent nature of their own theories, methods and models of inquiry. As educators we need to recognize the partiality of our own views in order to render them more suspect and open ended. We need to create the conditions and safe spaces that offer teachers and students the opportunity to be border crossers as part of the effort to learn new languages, refigure the boundaries of interdisciplinary discourse, and to constantly work to make the familiar strange and the given problematic.[5]

As a way of critiquing a notion of curriculum which takes a monolithic, quantifiable, stance towards education and learning in my book, I intend to argue for a pedagogical theory of curriculum based on a "curriculum of action," a theory that not only recognizes the importance of complexity and difference but, as Giroux advocates, also provides the condition for students to learn that the relationship between knowledge and power can be emancipatory, that their histories and experiences matter, and that what they say and do can count as part of a wider struggle to change the world around them.[6]

The relationship between language and action is critical in the attainment of power. The language that is available to us prioritizes a frame of reference within which we understand, reflect, name, and constitute our actions, feelings, and desires. The way we relate to language varies according to our diverse subjective possibilities, i.e., whether one is Asian or Caucasian, female or male, etc. Pedagogy, therefore, must involve itself in the practice of constituting meaning. This will allow it to create conditions that address discourse as a fluid domain in which lives can be transformed and liberated through an ongoing process of redefinition. The dynamic of the individual's relation to the social world presupposes that every individual plays a role in affecting the communication process. This, in existentialist terms, defines the individual's responsibility in the process of transformation and emancipation.

The philosophy of existentialism, because of the emphasis it places on concepts like freedom, responsibility, and choice, appeals to many educational philosophers.[7] The existentialist concept of freedom receives great emphasis in Maxine Greene's 1988 study, *Dialectic of Freedom*.[8] According to Greene, by acting upon their existential commitments, existentialist philosophers "have been concerned with moving persons to reflection upon themselves and to choose what to make of themselves within their own historical situations,"[9] whereby they arouse students to subjective awareness of their own lives. According to David Denton, Greene takes us to the heart of existentialism, especially in the opening of her essay "Literature, Existentialism and Education," where she discuses the importance of existential thinkers for literature and educational thought.[10] As she says, "Since 1842, when Soren Kierkegaard made indirect communication one of the categories of communication, existential philosophers have been awakening individuals to a sense of their condition through the use of literary devices and forms".[11] But Greene's interest is not only in Kierkegaard. She also considers the works of Friedrich Nietzsche, Albert Camus, Martin Buber, Simone de Beauvoir, Jean-Paul Sartre, Merleau-Ponty, and Hannah Arendt.

In light of the above argument concerning language, I will attempt in this book to elucidate Greene's existentialist concept of freedom as it relates to discourse embedded within a curriculum of action. Greene begins *Dialectic of Freedom* by stating that her "focal interest is in human freedom, in the capacity to surpass the given and look at things as if they could be otherwise."[12]

My project will attempt to illuminate and explain exactly how it is that Greene, by adopting the existentialist concept of freedom in action, creates a curriculum of empowerment for students, in which learning becomes the basis for challenging social practices that produce symbolic and real violence, making some students voiceless and thus powerless. It is important for Greene that through freedom, students must act to overcome the resistant realities that surround them. Once students overcome obstacles and imagine alternate possibilities, they must act to open up a public space wherein alternative possibilities may be named and in some instances actualized. This is why Greene says that that freedom is an achievement that occurs in the concreteness of lived situations.[13] She seems to accept what Sartre calls the "irreducibility of human praxis" and cites throughout the *Dialectic of Freedom* instances where genuine praxis appears in history.

Influenced by the language of praxis, my book, in critiquing back-to-basics and top-down schooling as premised on an inadequate definition of society, will suggest alternative ways of knowing, emphasizing possibility, hope, change, and freedom to this effect. Similar to critical theory, all thought, all consciousness in my work is intertwined with social processes and dialectics, continuing within it possibilities of what it might become, implying that the relationship between concept and object—between idea and the material world—is never still, never fixed, never absolutely certain.

Greene's work has certain important points of contact with the concerns of critical theory, and yet there are significant differences as well. I will discuss both in the following pages, beginning with Greene's essay "In Search of a Critical Pedagogy," where the similarities are more apparent. Here Greene asserts that, because the problems of education are profound and educators' notions of the possibilities for change are limited by a constrained discourse of modernity, it is often difficult even to envision more humane, more just, and more democratic alternatives. Greene's attention to context reminds us that critical pedagogy is not a one-size-fits-all methodology, but rather a process that must take into account social, political, and historical conditions. Yet without that vision, one cannot develop a critical pedagogy in which students resist materialism, conformity, and oppressive practices, and begin to think for themselves. To this effect, Greene grapples with ways of extracting and expanding the productive elements that emanated from the Age of Enlightenment—such as democracy and human rights—while eliminating the forms of domination that also accompanied this period.[14]

Greene shares with critical theorists a common emphasis on the centrality of the individual and the power of the individual endeavor, stressing the creative, active meaning-making aspects of men and women and seeing them as potentially free and capable of achieving their self-set goals. Both emphasize autonomy, creativity, and personal freedom. As a democratic mode of research, both seek to offer participants the capacity to examine their own practices, in turn offering them greater control over their own lives. The concept of theory at the heart of critical thinking and existentialist thought is therefore very different from that which has traditionally characterized educational studies. In the traditional view, theory has been applied to practice, and the two have been seen as distinct. Both critical theory and Greene's existentialist philosophy of action challenge this view, urging instead the fundamental indivisibility of theory and practice. Because of their commitment to emancipation, both argue that those whose lives are affected by decisions must have some influence over these decisions, some way of participating in making them. However, a fundamental problem of critical theory, which does not apply to Greene's existential philosophy, is its inability to break free from locating all social and educational ills in capitalism.

The assumption underlying the work of critical theorists is that no worthwhile curriculum improvement is possible without a radical transformation of social and political institutions, that abstract concepts like class, capitalism, and hegemony, which are, in some way, "real," provide the key to what is wrong with society. To this effect, they also stress possibility, hope, and change. But they perceive capitalism as the main problem in schools. Instances of this radical curriculum theory are reflected in the work of Michael Apple, Henry Giroux, Peter McLaren, and Christine Sleeter, among others.[15] These authors are often concerned with showing how the hidden curriculum of schooling reproduces the dominant relations of the workforce—how the patriarchal relations in the world of work are reflected in the organization of the school labor force, and how everything from this organization to the production and circulation of textbooks is governed by the principles of political economy.[16] The focus here is primarily political and ideological; its emphasis is on highlighting how schools function to reproduce, in both the hidden and the formal curricula, the cultural beliefs and economic relationships that support the larger social order.[17]

Because the above-mentioned critical thinking-based teaching is derived from an ideological position in that the values of rationality, clarity, and predictability are assumed, the emphasis on social reproduction has the effect of turning teaching into a technique for controlling behavior and ignoring those aspects of the teaching relationship that are fundamentally existential in nature. Philosophical questions about the relationship between education and the future of students are simply ignored. Although critical theorists embrace the terminology of possibility, what is striking, especially in Apple's case, is the absence of any sustained effort to describe the kind of structural conditions (i.e., the objective conditions of possibility) that would open up the way for the effective emergence of democratic forces.[18]

Although critical theorists oppose dominant social, cultural, and educational paradigms, their work has had little effect on what they describe as a misanthropic social system, segregated according to class, race, and gender. Critical theorists may urge American schools to produce a more democratic community, but they seldom speak with one voice on a program for social/political change. Possibly, they lack answers to the problems they pose. Moreover, by avoiding questions of experience and existential agency, these writers fail to provide a program for transformation that would enable educators to move from their current despair to concrete strategies for change.

Greene's work differs from critical theory in its emphasis on purpose. The goal of Greene's work is to suggest changes in the structure and governance of schools that will eliminate the dehumanizing effect of school routine, while at the same time ensuring that students can begin to explore the interface between their own existential questions and the assumptions that underlie their sociocultural milieu. Consequently, Greene's pedagogy, which is limited by the constraints of philosophical interrogation, does not concern itself with questions such as supervision or the norms and control of the efficiency of educational systems. In fact, it would not be able to quantify the efficiency of dialogue in the classroom. It is instead a slow movement of self-renewal, a result of practical engagement and not just of mental exercises in which existential teachers create conditions and require students to discover the answer themselves.

Central to a realizable critical pedagogy that Greene envisions is the need to view schools as democratic public spheres. Consequently, any attempt to reformulate the role of educators has to begin with the broader question of how to view existentialist schooling. Consequently, too, a strategy that takes curriculum change seriously would need to base itself on another approach, one that looks at curriculum issues from an existentialist point of view with respect to freedom.

The objective of my work is concerned with examining this existential curriculum of freedom. The reality of life as interpreted in my project consists neither of classes, capitalism, and hegemony nor of administrative processes and established structures, but is limited to the relationships of persons as participants in a community, at various intersections of gender, class, ethnicity and other differences. In interpreting the existentialist concept of human freedom as embodied in the work of Maxine Greene, my research will be limited to a qualitative analysis of existentialist pedagogy. This interpretation, in turn, will be limited to my own perspective on Greene's work, with no claim to finality of conclusions or to having accounted for all that has been or might be said about this author.

Chapter One begins with an elucidation Sartre's influence on Greene's existentialist concept of freedom. By comparing the concepts of freedom in *Be-*

ing and Nothingness[19] and *Dialectic of Freedom*, I will show how Greene, by incorporating certain aspects of Sartre's concept of freedom, contextualizes freedom within a dynamic concept of action. The purpose of this chapter will be to show how Greene, by locating her concept of freedom within a Sartrean interpretation, explores the implications such a grounding would have for educators.

Further elaborating Greene's concept of action as it relates to freedom, I will proceed in Chapter Two to show how Greene builds on Sartre's notions of action and freedom to create an educational theory of emancipation. This chapter will emphasize how Greene clearly aligns herself with Merleau-Ponty in her emphasis on intersubjectivity and on the "mutual exchanges that forge communities".[20] As for Merleau-Ponty, freedom for Greene is both a public as well as a personal achievement. To this extent Merleau-Ponty's influence on Greene will be examined, especially as it manifests itself in what Greene refers to as "social imagination."

I will then go on to examine what the concept of freedom gains from this development, and what therefore places Green above Sartre and others involved in the freedom discourse. Greene's advantage lies in her interpretation of freedom within an educational setting. She takes the theoretical discussion of existentialist freedom a step further by implementing it concretely in curriculum discourse, a topic otherwise largely foreign to the freedom discourse.

Within this educational context, for Greene, "to make sense means to liberate oneself,"[21] a concept she credits to Paulo Freire. Freedom for Freire, as for Greene, requires both reflection and action, both interpretation and change, and cultural action for freedom is characterized by dialogue, specifically by the act of naming. With situations opening, students may become empowered to engage in some sort of praxis, engaged enough to name the obstacles in the way of their shared becoming.[22] Once students begin to name the world, they transform, through their own actions, their individual lives. The challenge for Greene, as it is for Freire, is to engage as many young people as possible to name their world, thus motivating them toward collective action.[23] For both writers, the inability to articulate interferes with the process of education and learning. Insofar as students are submerged in the voices of power that control them, they are unable to critically reinterpret their surroundings and recognize the various vantage points.[24] Education, for both Greene and Freire, is vital in this process. As part of my discussion, I will undertake a thorough examination of Greene's concept of naming as influenced by Freire.[25]

Chapter Three will further elucidate how the positive role of "possibility,"as interpreted within the realm of education, is manifested in Greene's discussion of literature. In Greene's view, imaginative literature holds significance for the existential philosopher above all because of its dominating interest in human freedom. Works of literature offer this possibility to the student as well. In this chapter, I will emphasize how Greene, through her use of literary texts, creates a space for freedom and possibility to exist simultaneously.

In light of Greene's literary curriculum of action and naming, I will explore in Chapter Four alternative curricula that emphasize dialogical knowing, thinking, and experiencing on the basis of creating a new language of open and decentered spaces—curricula that do not confine individuals and students under the umbrella of standardization, but instead celebrate individual multiplicities within a plurality of meanings.

The humanistic interpretation of the curriculum will be discussed with special attention to the influences of educators like Max van Manen, William Pinar, and Madeline Grumet. Although these authors support the critical theorists' critique of the dehumanizing process of schooling, they extend this critique into a "mode for articulating and reading texts of educational experience that locates alternative discussion for curriculum within the daily experience of teachers and students."[26] Challenging the prevalence of quantitative methods of inquiry and of education, this chapter will elucidate how these thinkers explicate the humanities and the traditions of philosophy and literature that use narratives to order as well as to express experience. Pinar, drawing on the philosophy of Jacques Derrida and on psychoanalytic theories, argues that debates about what is taught to young children are "debates about who we perceive ourselves to be and how we will present that identity".[27] He argues that a curriculum project should seek to recover memory, to understand how the systems of reasoning and categories of inclusion have raised "the other" as different from what is perceived and classified as "normal." As opposed to standardization of the quantitative research model, the emphasis here is on the biography of the individual writer, on the adequacy of everyday experience as a context for knowledge, and on the capacity of the narrative form to contain and convey the character of educational experience.[28] Viewed from this perspective, education emerges as a metaphor for a person's dialogue with the world of his or her experience.

By incorporating Greene's educational pedagogy into a curriculum of action, my concluding Chapter Five will attempt to show how educational leaders and classroom teachers can concretely implement and develop an existentialist curriculum in their classroom which, as Sartre would have it, is grounded in the vision of leadership and freedom and embodies a language of both critique and possibility, one that represents both a "flight and a leap ahead, at once refusal and realization".[29]

Finally, then, the aim of my book is to create an existentialist curriculum, one that embodies the student's right to examine his or her culture without being punished if he or she does not reach the conclusions legitimated by the dominant society. The purpose of any teaching must be to help students develop the intellectual and critical skills they need to become active, intelligent, and informed citizens, and any methodology that forces students to uncritically absorb someone else's idea of what is important is antithetical to the democratic goal. A fundamental issue that pedagogy of a concrete curriculum of action should take up is therefore the need to conceptualize the appropriation of new discourses as a process of learning languages, languages that allow not only access to different ways of thinking, but also to the reconceptualization of problems. Hopefully by creating alternative curriculum discourses and alternative ways to assess educational standards educators and curriculum theorists can view curriculum in a situated context.

NOTES

1. Robert Williams Connel, "Poverty and Education," *Harvard Educational Review* 64/2 (Summer 1994): 137.

2. Connel, 137.

3. Theodore Sizer, *Horace's Compromise: The Dilemma of the American High School* (Boston: Houghton Mifflin, 1984), 237.

4. Henry A. Giroux, *Living Dangerously: Multiculturalism and the Politics of Difference* (New York: Peter Lang Press, 1993), 23.

5. Henry Giroux, *Multiculturalism and the Politics of Difference* (New York: Peter Lang Publishing Inc., 1993), 25.

6. Giroux, *Multiculturalism and the Politics of Difference*, 245.

7. Khemais Benhabiba, "Sartre's Existentialism and Education: The Missing Foundation of Human Relations," *Educational Theory* 23/3 (Summer 1973).

8. Maxine Greene, *Dialectic of Freedom* (New York: Teachers College Press, 1988).

9. Maxine Greene, "Literature, Existentialism and Education," in *Existentialism and Phenomenology in Education: Collected Essays*, ed. David E. Denton (New York: Teachers College Press, 1974), 65.

10. Denton, *Existentialism and Phenomenology in Education: Collected Essays*, 63.

11. Greene, "Literature, Existentialism and Education," 63.

12. Greene, *Dialectic of Freedom*, 3.

13. Greene, *Dialectic of Freedom*, 4–5.

14. Maxine Greene, "In Search of a Critical Pedagogy," in *The Transformative Power of Critical Pedagogy*, eds. Pepi Leistyna, Arlie Woodrum, and Stephen A. Sherblum, (Cambridge, Mass.: Harvard Educational Review, 1996), 13.

15. Michael W. Apple, *Ideology and Curriculum* (New York: Routledge, 1979); Henry Giroux, *Border Crossings: Cultural Workers and the Politics of Education*

(New York: Routledge, 1992); Peter L. McLaren, "Critical Pedagogy: Constructing an Arch of Social Dreaming and a Doorway to Hope," *Journal of Education* (1992); Sonia Nieto, *Affirming Diversity: The Sociopolitical Context of Multicultural Education*, 2nd ed. (New York: Longman, 1995); Christine E. Sleeter, & P. McLaren, eds., *Multicultural Education, Critical Pedagogy and the Politics of Discourse* (Albany: State University of New York Press, 1995).

16. Michael Apple, "Series Editor's Introduction," *Capitalist Schools*, ed. D. Liston (New York: Routledge, 1988).

17. For a further discussion see p. 102 curriculum and instruction.

18. Morrow and Torres, 331.

19. Jean Paul Sartre, *Being and Nothingness*, trans. Hazel E. Barnes (New York: Philosophical Library, 1956).

20. W. Ayers, "Interview with Maxine Greene," *Qualitative Studies in Education* 8/4 (1995), 319328.

21. Maxine Greene, *Teacher as Stranger: Educational Philosophy for the Modern Age* (California: Wadsworth Publishing Company, 1973), 163.

22. Greene, *Dialectic of Freedom*, 133.

23. Greene, *Dialectic of Freedom*, 125.

24. Greene, *Dialectic of Freedom*, 132.

25. Paulo Freire, *Pedagogy of the Oppressed* (New York: Seabury Press, 1968).

26. Madeline R. Grumet, *Bitter Milk: Women and Education* (Amherst: The University of Massachusetts Press, 1988), 60.

27. William F. Pinar, "Notes on Understanding Curriculum as a Racial Text," in *Race, Identity and Representation in Education*, ed. Cameron McCarthy and Warren Crichlow (London: Routledge Press, 1993), 60.

28. Madeline Grumet, "Existential and Phenomenological Foundations of Autobiographical Methods," in *Understand Curriculum a Phenomenological and Deconstructed Text*, eds. William. F. Pinar and William M. Reynolds (New York: Teachers College Press, 1992), 28.

29. Jean Paul Sartre, *Search for a Method* (New York: Alfred A. Knopf, 1963), 92.

Chapter One

Sartre and Greene: Contextualizing Freedom in Action

Soren Kierkegaard,[1] the father of modern existentialism, believed that Socrates pointed the way to existentialist techniques for communicating the truth. In *Courage to Be*,[2] Paul Tillich provides a guideline for understanding the role played by existentialists in western thought: existentialism, according to Tillich, is a philosophy that emerges from spiritual crises. Historically, there have been situations that have forced people to profoundly doubt their belief in themselves, in nature, or in their gods. When one senses the pressure of one's own death, the guilt for one's deeds, or the pointlessness of one's life, one is ripe for the development of existentialist ideas.

Jean-Paul Sartre believed that what separates existentialist thought from other philosophies was best expressed in the maxim, "Existence precedes essence." "Essence" for Sartre refers to that of which a thing or being is intrinsically made, while "existence" refers to the act by which it came about and is. Existentialism, which positions human existence at the center of the world, believes that the real world (reality) is the world of existing. Therefore, to the existentialist, existence must involve action; this means that one exists, in the existentialist sense of the term, to the degree that one engages oneself in the world and creates one's own destiny. To be human within this context is to freely chose one's own a situation, to risk oneself in choice, and to commit oneself to one's choice and to the consequences of that choice. Freedom within such an existentialist context is intelligible in the sense that it is brought into the world by human action, and a theory of freedom has therefore to take into account the theory of human action.

Nel Noddings in her book, *Philosophy and Education*[3] says that Maxine Greene clearly locates herself in the existentialist tradition when she rejects the notion of a system that confers freedom on its members. In a related quote Greene says:

> I believe it unthinkable any longer for Americans to assert themselves to be 'free' because they belong to a free country. Not only do we need to be continually empowered to choose ourselves, to create our identities within a plurality; we need continually to make new promises and to act in our freedom to fulfill them, something we can never do alone.[4]

Freedom, then, cannot mean autonomous achievement. Since we are situated in a community, freedom for Greene, as for Dewey, is an achievement that occurs in the concreteness of lived social situations.[5] Greene refers in this connection to Dewey's own statement: "Social conditions interact with the preferences of an individual—in a way favorable to actualizing freedom only when they develop intelligence, not abstract knowledge and abstract thought, but power of vision and reflection".

But Greene's existentialist methodology is concerned with examining subjectivity, imagination, and human freedom, usually the province of diaries, letters, confessions, poems, novels, and plays. Greene's concern is not with the objective and universal, but with the subjective and individualistic concept of freedom, a concern Greene echoes from Sartre.[6] In keeping with Sartre's existentialist thinking, the essence of individuality, for Greene, includes exploring the reflexive nature of selfhood, wherein the self relates itself to itself, which makes possible knowledge of oneself. According to Greene, Sartre saw human beings as creating themselves by going beyond what exists, by trying to bring something into being.[7] And the freedom to do this can be achieved only in an ongoing transaction, one that is visible to those involved. We must never forget that "there is always more, there is always possibility, and this is where the pursuit opens for the language of freedom".[8]

Consequently, in order to understand Greene's concept of freedom, it becomes imperative to examine Sartre's existentialist concept of freedom and to elucidate the similarities between the two. In this chapter, I will discuss the relevance of Sartre's existentialist concept of action in understanding Greene's concept of freedom. In elaborating Sartre's concept of freedom and action as it is developed in Greene, I will examine the existential application of this method in her educational philosophy. The purpose of this chapter is to illustrate how Greene's concept of freedom is contextualized within an existentialist tradition and influenced by Sartre's concept of freedom as elucidated in *Being and Nothingness*.[9] Given the extensive and complex nature of Sartre's philosophical project, it is both necessary and appropriate that I limit the present discussion to those aspects of Sartre's philosophy that relate directly to freedom, and in particular to those aspects which have had a direct influence on Greene.

The main tenet of Greene's philosophy lies in freedom. In *The Dialectic of Freedom*, Greene explores the variety of ways in which human beings have construed freedom. The emphasis for Greene, in keeping with the existentialist tradition, is on the self. To speak of the self, according to Greene, is to "speak of an individual's body as well as his/her mind, his past as well as his present; the world in which he is involved and the others with whom he is continually engaged".[10] According to Greene, social action comes by opening perspectives. As she explains, "We might think of freedom as opening of spaces as well as perspectives, with everything depending on the actions we undertake in the course of our quest, the praxis we learn to devise".[11] In fact, Greene suggests that, for educators, the "problem is not simply to interpret the world . . . the point, as Marx wrote . . . is to *change* it".[12]

Freedom for Greene is "the capacity to identify openings in situations, possible courses of action".[13] Greene goes on to say that one way in which freedom can be attained is "through the refusals . . . of which Sartre spoke".[14] According to Greene, for "Jean-Paul Sartre, the project of acting on our freedom involves a rejection of the insufficient or the unendurable, a clarification, an imagining of a better state of things".[15] Similarly, Greene believes that it is only after a "crisis of consciousness"[16] that people act; when situations become unbearable, action occurs.[17]

The concept of freedom for both Sartre and Greene, and for the latter via the former, is grounded in the understanding that the subject depends on something outside its own existence to complete itself. For both, too, consciousness is always consciousness of something other than itself.[18] According to Sartre, an action "is on principle intentional".[19] All the intentions of consciousness are directed outside itself. Consciousness for Sartre has no meaning by itself, since it manifests itself as a desire for some object in the world; the world in turn has no intrinsic meaning, since it has to be intended by human consciousness or human desire.

In keeping with Sartre's existentialist philosophy, dialectical processes for Greene are also created anew through intentional action. We as human beings apprehend the world dialectically. Greene begins her *Dialectic of Freedom* by declaring: "This book arises out of a lifetime preoccupation with quest, with pursuit." We are first told that the quest is deeply "personal, that is, a woman striving to affirm the feminine as wife, mother, friend, while reaching, always reaching, beyond the limits imposed by the obligations of a woman's life".[20] On the other hand, we are told that the question is "deeply public" as well, "that of a person struggling to connect the undertaking of education, with which she has been so long involved, making and remaking of a public space, a space of dialogue and possibility." Thus, we are at once introduced to one of the major dialectics within the "dialectic of freedom:" that between the personal and the public, self and society, subjectivity and objectivity.

To speak of a dialectic is for Greene to speak of forces in contest—Greene defines "dialectics" as the factors that hold us in place, that stand in the way of our growing, and that provoke us to act on our desires, to break through obstacles, to become different, to be.[21] According to Greene a dialectic relation marks every situation, including the relations between subject and object, individual and environment, self and society, outsider and community, living consciousness and the phenomenal world. This relation exists between two extremes, and yet it identifies a mediation between them. Take, for example, the relation between choosing, moving beyond oneself, and the object, whether an artificial or a natural organism or a construction. One comes in touch with an object, such as a table, by grasping it through an act of consciousness. The function of the object is clear to the extent that one recognizes the table and sees a similarity between it and tables known and used in one's past. Yet the reality of the table emerges only in the course of one's encounter with it, based on one's interpreted experience with the table and with similar tables, as it is thematized and symbolized by language, which is to say by naming. This is what is suggested by mediation: "something that occurs between culture, nature, work and action . . . freedom achieved can only involve a surpassing of determinateness".[22]

The dialectical projects of *Being and Nothingness* and *Dialectic of Freedom* refer in part to the human capacity to harbor desires with respect to entities that are not present. This capacity to experience absence or negativity is also the capacity to annihilate the given or to withdraw from it. We are conscious of an absence as a lack in our lives. Sartre states:

> Human reality is its own surpassing toward what it lacks; it surpasses itself toward the particular being which it would be if it were what it is. Human reality is not something which exists first in order afterwards to lack this or that; it exists first as lack in immediate, synthetic connection with what it lacks. . . . In its coming into existence human reality grasps itself as an incomplete being. It apprehends itself as being in so far as it is not, in the presence of the particular totality which it lacks and which it is in the form of not being it and which is what it is. Human reality is a perpetual surpassing toward a coincidence with itself which is never given.[23]

Consciousness by way of experiencing a certain negativity, an objective absence of a certain value, is the activity of withdrawing from the present and negating it. The past exists because it was once annihilated by a certain activity of consciousness. Consequently, human reality for Sartre is a project

? You are what you perceive yourself to be—once you see you are not—you are forever striving for + toward it b/c it was always "you"

that lives in the present by negating the past, so that what will be can come only by not being what it is. The present for Sartre is not the nature of consciousness, as consciousness is never defined by what it is. It always goes beyond the present. So consciousness is never something that remains fixed, permanent. It always transcends toward an unfolding future.[24]

Similarly, for Greene, consciousness is never static. As she herself states,

> There has to be a surpassing of a constraining or deficient 'reality,' actually perceived as deficient by a person or persons looking from their particular vantage points on the world. Made conscious of lacks, they may move (in their desire to repair them) towards a 'field of possibilities,' what is possible or realizable for them.[25]

Consequently, for Greene, the relationship between freedom and human consciousness is one of action. Praxis for Greene, following Sartre, is "a flight, a leap, at once a refusal and a realization."[26]

This realization and refusal is for both Sartre and Greene a permanent human possibility, allowing us to wrench ourselves away from the presently given determinants to that of an absent being. And it is only against the background of a future possibility that one realizes the present lack. As Sartre states in *Being and Nothingness*, "I project myself toward the Future in order to merge there with that which I lack; that is, with that which if synthetically added to my Present would make me what I am".[27] Individual motivation for action then comes from positing a possible state of affairs in the future. And only through positing a future goal can the present world be judged and the present social arrangements appear as an obstacle or aid.

The temporal movement of the future is also the cornerstone of Greene's concept of freedom. In *The Dialectic of Freedom*, Greene defines concrete freedom as "an act by which a human being orients oneself to the future, of struggling to overcome limits that define one's actions, situatedness, of moving beyond in the full awareness that such overcoming can never be complete".[28] And in a direct reference to Sartre, Greene says, "As I write of social imagination I am reminded of Jean-Paul Sartre's declaration that it is on the day that we conceive of a different state of affairs that a new light falls on our troubles and our suffering and that we decide that these are unbearable".[29] She goes on to say that "it should remind us of the relation between freedom and the consciousness of possibility, between freedom and imagination—the ability to make present what is absent, to summon up a condition of what is not yet".[30] Consequently, human reality for Greene is concretely expressed by a transcendence toward what it lacks. This transcendence is manifested in the projects of individual human consciousness, its movement, as it were, toward its possibilities.

constantly re-inventing oneself

According to Greene, recognition of one's freedom is "a matter of being able to envisage things as they could be otherwise, or of positing alternatives to mere passivity".[31] Resignation for Greene, again via Sartre, implies failure to act on one's freedom. When we resign ourselves to a situation, even if it is done voluntarily, we do so because we don't experience any negativity or any alternate vision of reality. When an alternate vision is missing, oppressive conditions become natural and we accept our lot. But these conditions are not sufficient to bring about action. Such conditions must be recognized as unbearable when judged in the light of an alternate project.

This human possibility to negate and reject, surpass and transcend, is what Sartre and Greene call freedom. A human being's surpassing toward his or her possibilities consists in awareness of his or her freedom. Freedom in this context is thought of as being reflective and self-aware. One's choice breaks the chain of causes and effects, of probabilities in which one normally feels oneself to be entangled. One breaks this chain in part by asking why, by perceiving the habitual itself to be an obstacle to one's growth, one's pursuit of meaning, one's interpreting and naming of one's world. There must be a why, a sense of impasse, an immediate sense of obstacle. If a person is to be moved to act on his or her possibilities, to perceive what might be, choice is never automatic. The individual, aware of being blocked in some way, must posit the situation as one in which there are alternatives as well as obstacles to be overcome. For this, he or she must have the capacity to reflect on the situation in its concreteness. Freedom within such a context is sought, according to Greene, "only when what presses down (or conditions or limits) is perceived as an obstacle . . . where people cannot name alternatives or imagine a better state of things, they are likely to remain anchored or submerged".[32] The point Greene is making is that human beings who break with the ordinary mechanical life need to be awake to conditions and consequences—to be able to diagnose impinging circumstances in the everyday and to identify the likely consequences of the actions they undertake.

Thus, the dialectic of freedom emerges as a result of many reinforcing dialectics. The first freedom is always the awakening of the imagination that posits alternate realities. In his essay, "Greene's Dialectics of Freedom and Dewey's Naturalistic Existential Metaphysics," James E. Garrison says that all these dialectics are defined within a public space circumscribed by the dialects between self and society, the individual and the community.[33] According to Greene, one's reality, rather than being fixed and predefined, is perpetually emerging, becoming increasingly multiplex as more perspectives are taken, more texts are opened, and more friendships are made.[34] The dialectic of freedom, according to Greene, then "emerges out of the dialectic of the actual and potential, the subject and object, the necessary and the possible, the real and the imagined".[35] Of these, I turn in what follows to the freedom of choice.

Greene believes that unless and until we can posit and imagine alternative possibilities we have no freedom, regardless of how unfettered we might feel. Suppression of the imagination, in fact, may be the greatest oppression. But a free imagination, freedom of thought, is not enough to fully secure personal or public freedom. To be free it is necessary to engage in those actualities that bind us.[36] Freedom in the positive sense requires first imagining alternatives, then naming what oppresses us, followed by action to secure some named object of our desire. Freedom without choice is meaningless.

It is this theme of human freedom that is central to Sartre's and Greene's dialectical philosophies. Their shared conception of consciousness as a function of negation and transcendence is indicative of human freedom. The core of the theory of freedom exists for both within this intentionality of chosen purpose. For both, too, the theory of intentionality claims that the relationship of consciousness (subject to object) is not destined by a first cause. In human beings, there are no ultimate ends common to all men and women. Each individual chooses his or her own end and can adapt new ones, even ends diametrically opposed to past ones.

According to Sartre, an individual's ability to reflect gives him or her the freedom to choose his or her own destination—within limits. One's reflective capacity enables one to give meaning to things and events. Only in retrospect can an individual identify his or her conscious acts and place value judgments on them. Thus, Sartre concludes that "the world gives council only if one questions it [and] only for a well determined end".[37] Reasons, then, are relative to ends; but the ends are constituted by the projects of each individual consciousness. These resistances or obstacles to freedom Sartre and Greene call *facticity*. As seen above, an obstacle exists as such because there is a human reality that conceives it as an obstacle in the light of the project or end it has undertaken. Therefore, what is an obstacle for one individual, Sartre says, "may not be so for another". He goes on to say that a *you create your own obstacles by deciding that they are*

rock will not be an obstacle if I wish at any cost to arrive at the top of the mountain. On the other hand, it will discourage me if I have freely fixed limits on my desire of making the projected climb. Thus the world reveals to me the way in which I stand in relation to the ends which I assign myself.[38] *You set your own limits.*

A mountain, using Sartre's example, is to me too difficult to climb, but only so because it is conceived as unclimbable. An example of this external facticity is the mountain that just happens to be blocking the route to the town that I want to reach. The mountain is a fact that I cannot wish away. As fact, it poses an obstacle to my decision to reach the town in a certain time. I can always remove its force as obstacle by deciding to go to a different town, but I cannot remove the mountain; nor can I remove its resistance to my initial decisions. Facticity, then, clearly poses resistance. To put it another way, resistance is intrinsic to freedom and humanness.[39] Freedom is consequently meaningful only in the context of obstacles and resistance, and arises in the face of resistance.

Similarly, concrete human freedom for Greene is conceived as the "autonomy of choice"[40] in relation to a resistant world that is actual and independent of human consciousness. In her commitment to existentialism, Greene also insists upon the agency of individuals and the possibility for freedom brought about by choice and by action as one recognizes and confronts the reality of external conditions.[41] In a direct reference to Sartre, Greene goes on to say that "As Sartre saw it, human beings create themselves by going beyond what exists, by trying to bring something into being".[42] According to Greene, it is important to affirm that it is always the individual, acting voluntarily in a particular situation at a particular moment, who does the deciding.[43] Therefore, a conscious engagement in an action (or endeavor to realize a project) is for Greene something that must be intentionally sustained by a choice or a decision that is an expression of "existential freedom."

Recognizing the importance of such voluntary choice, Greene emphasizes its role:

> In the bulk of existentialist literature, there is a fundamental respect for reasoning as well as reflection, for experience as well as subjectivity. The existentialists may deny the primacy of knowledge, as Sartre does when he talks about self-consciousness and the discovery of the being of the knower; but he will also vehemently challenge (as Sartre also does) someone who becomes an anti-semite because he is impervious to reason and reflection.[44]

In other words, voluntary deliberation for Greene is necessary for action. Despite the obstacles one encounters in action (climbing a mountain), one in the end *chooses* to yield to fatigue, to rest, to abandon the project. The negation of the fulfillment of a project is always a theoretical possibility for Greene. She desires, at all costs, to preserve the notion of our responsibility for our sustained project or its abandonment. In effect, she is concerned to emphasize the individual's responsibility for his or her actions and for the ways in which he or she names the world. This, too, Greene credits to Sartre for whom she says that individuals

> do not reach out for fulfillment if they don't feel impeded somehow, and if they are not enabled to *name* the obstacles that stand in their way. At once the very

existence of obstacles depends on the desire to reach toward wider spaces for fulfillment, to expand options, to know alternatives. As has been said, a rock is an obstacle only to the one who wants to climb the hill. Not caring the traveler may seek another path.[45]

Similarly, for Greene, before human beings even begin to define and redefine themselves by overcoming obstacles and creating possibilities, it is crucial that they perceive the "obstacles" as obstacles to be overcome. Human beings must take the natural as a given. Action in this context means beginning or taking initiatives to overcome obstacles or resistances, because, as Greene says, "Only by means of such resistance, I discovered, can we widen the spaces in which we hope to choose ourselves. To meet a wall or a barrier in our way and simply to take another path is to acquiesce, not to resist".[46]

But this choosing, for Sartre and thus also for Greene, does not come without cost. It is this aspect of human freedom that for humanity is the source of anguish. The idea of this fundamental attitude thus involves responsibility. Human beings, according to Sartre, are the authors of the world. The world, in turn, is human freedom; it is what they make of it. Individuals carry "the weight of the whole world on their shoulders, they are responsible for the world, and for themselves as a way of being".[47]

Anguish, for Sartre, is then the human attitude toward freedom. As Sartre says, "Anguish then is the reflective apprehension of freedom by itself".[48] Anguish occurs because one can actively pursue options that are not imposed from the outside. It is the apprehension of the self acting on a situation. Human beings face anguish when they recognize their freedom, when they recognize that there is no absoluteness, only uncertainty. What is right today can be wrong tomorrow, as different appearances shine forth. There is anguish because a human being realizes that it is only he or she who is responsible for his or her actions, since he or she (as known through implications of consciousness) is the one by "whom it happens that there is a world".[49] Thus, anguish arises because, though one is not the foundation of one's being, everything takes place as if one were compelled to be responsible. In other words, one is abandoned in a world that is, abandoned to a freedom from which one cannot escape. This freedom is compulsion to derive the meaning of being—within it, and everywhere outside of it. Therefore, anguish, according to Sartre, is a reflective comprehension of freedom by itself. It arises from the negations or appeals of the world.

It is also through the process of "anguish," Greene asserts, that "freedom reveals itself. It is the expression of the nagging desire for completion— without any guarantee that the completion sought will be valuable when it is achieved".[50] Moreover, "it is in this dreadful freedom that the individual decides to confront his (her) own freedom, his (her) own need to choose".[51] Consequently, for Green, the individual suffers from disquietude.

↑ worried/unease

*Constantly recreating thru freedom to choose
ones own path - responsibly*

In a further discussion of anguish, Greene says that an individual is always "in situation:"

> His self emerges in projects, in undertakings; it does not pre-exist. His acts are free acts, he is dreadfully free to make of himself, at every moment, something other than what he is. Fearful though it is (Because 'anything is possible'), the individual's freedom is finite. He may perceive multiple possibilities, but he can choose only against the background of necessity. Everyone has a past, a family, an environment; teachers, like other working people and professionals, are controlled or limited by 'givens' connected with their jobs. These suggest only some of the necessities that must somehow be synthesized with possibility. The problem for the individual is to transform necessity into freedom by taking responsibility for it, acting toward the future rather than the past.[52]

Therefore, anguish for Greene prevents a human being from being enchained to his or her possibilities. The past of human reality is closed, its present a perpetual flight and its future eternally problematic. It is because human reality is free that it can transcend its past and present toward its future, but its freedom is also a painful limit that leaves it eternally restless.

Freedom and situation turn out to be correlative. Conditions, moreover, are not obstacles to freedom but the basis of freedom. Since one's facticity or consciousness is always rooted in a factual situation, it is across one's body that one is aware of the object. Thus, the body is conceived as an instrumental center where action originates. Bodily consciousness hinges on factual situations, and is therefore without content. Each situation in the world is different, and identity is in turn dependent upon each different situation.

For Sartre, then, freedom is paradoxical; it exists only in a situation, and the situation is only constituted through freedom.[53] The totality of human reality is impossible to attain; human beings try to assume an identity on which they can base their actions on, and assumes the responsibility of reacting to every situation according to that identity. This for Sartre is impossible, because individuals are never fixed in a static identity and therefore cannot treat every situation under this assumption. Human reality by nature, then, is unhappy consciousness, because there is no possibility of surpassing its unhappy state. As Sartre says:

> The being of human reality is suffering because it arises in being perpetually haunted by a totality which it is without being able to be it. . . . Human reality therefore is by nature unhappy consciousness.[54]

This unhappiness is the result of an individual's paradoxical desire, as the ideal of totality always haunts consciousness, which it can neither attain nor give up. Greene, on the other hand, invites us to do philosophy with a desired goal—to become aware of our possibilities.

In conclusion, I have attempted in this chapter to show how, elaborating on certain aspects of Sartre's concept of freedom, Greene develops an existentialist notion of choice where she encourages human beings to recognize their freedom by making them pose problems and refer those problems to contexts of action. But in the next chapter I want to elucidate how Greene takes Sartre a step further when she recontextualizes aspects of his philosophy to the sphere of American education, a sphere which for her is intrinsically social. The main assumption underlying Greene's book, *The Dialectic of Freedom* is one of intersubjectivity. Elaborating on Merleau-Ponty's notion of the dialectic which is inexorably bound to the world and intertwined within a social context[55], Greene offers us possible ways in which we are encouraged to struggle with ideas, art, and events of the world—all in order to become more aware of ourselves and of our world, more aware of our intersubjective predicament and, more importantly, able to act on our awareness. In the next chapter, I will examine how Greene carries this dialectical project forward.

intersubjectivity - ? within ones conscious self?

NOTES   *interaction b/t 2 people*

1. David E. Denton, ed., *Existentialism and Phenomenology in Education: Collected Essays* (New York: Teachers College Press, 1974), 2238.
2. Paul Tillich, *Courage to Be* (New Haven, Conn.: Yale University Press, 1952).
3. Nel Noddings, *Philosophy and Education: Dimensions of Philosophy Series* (Boulder, Colo.: Westview Press, 1995) 62
4. Maxine Greene, *Dialectic of Freedom*, (New York: Teachers College Press, 1988) 51
5. Greene, *Dialectic of Freedom*, 4–5.
6. Maxine Greene, *Teacher as Stranger: Educational Philosophy for the Modern Age*, (Belmont, Calif.: Wadsworth Publishing Company, 1973) 137.
7. Greene, *Dialectic of Freedom*, 22.
8. Ibid., 128.
9. Jean-Paul Sartre, *Being and Nothingness: An Essay on Phenomenological Ontology*, trans. Hazel Barnes (New York: The Philosophical Library, 1956).
10. Greene, *Teacher as Stranger*, 136.
11. Greene, *Dialectic of Freedom*, 5.
12. Maxine Greene, *Landscapes of Learning*, (New York: Teachers College, 1978) 109.
13. Ibid., 221.
14. Ibid., 9.

15. Greene, *Dialectic of Freedom*, 5.

16. Greene, *Teacher as Stranger*, 268.

17. Marla Morris, "Existential and Phenomenological Influences on Maxine Greene" in William F. Pinar, ed., *The Passionate Mind of Maxine Greene: "I am . . . not Yet* (London: Falmer Press, 1998), 130.

18. Sartre, *Being and Nothingness*, 1i.

19. Ibid., 433.

20. Greene, *Dialectic of Freedom*, xi.

21. Maxine Greene, *Releasing the Imagination: Essays on Education, Arts, and Social Change* (San Francisco: Jossey-Bass Publishers, 1995), 112.

22. Greene, *Dialectic of Freedom*, 8.

23. Sartre, *Being and Nothingness*, 89.

24. For a detailed discussion on this topic, see Sartre, *Being and Nothingness*, Part 2, Chapter 2, "Temporality."

25. Greene, *Dialectic of Freedom*, 5.

26. Jean-Paul Sartre, *Search for a Method*, trans. Hazel E. Barnes (New York: Vintage Books, 1968), 98.

27. Sartre, *Being and Nothingness*, 127.

28. Greene, *Dialectic of Freedom*, 5.

29. Greene, *Releasing the Imagination*, 5, from Sartre, *Being and Nothingness*, 4345.

30. Greene, *Releasing the Imagination*, 5.

31. Greene, *Dialectic of Freedom*, 16.

32. Greene, *Releasing the Imagination*, 52.

33. James E. Garrison, "Greene's Dialectics of Freedom and Dewey's Naturalistic Existential Metaphysics," in *Educational Theory* 40/2 (Spring 1990), 201.

34. Greene, *Dialectic of Freedom*, 23.

35. Ibid. 21

36. 199

37. Sartre, *Being and Nothingness*, 448.

38. Sartre, *Being and Nothingness*, 488–9.

39. Ibid., 453–5.

40. Ibid., 483.

41. See Wendy Kohli, "Philosopher of/for Freedom," in *A Light in Dark Times: Maxine Greene and the Unfinished Conversation* (New York: Teachers College Press, 1998), 17.

42. Greene, *Dialectic of Freedom*, 22.

43. Greene, *Landscapes of Learning*, 49.

44. Greene, *Teacher as Stranger*, 138.

45. Greene, *Dialectic of Freedom*, 5.

46. Greene, *Releasing the Imagination*, 112.

47. Sartre, *Being and Nothingness*, 553.

48. Ibid., 38.

49. Jean-Paul Sartre, *Existentialism and Human Emotion*, trans. Barnard Frechtman and Hazel Barnes (New York: Citadel Press, 1977), 55.

50. Greene, *Teacher as Stranger*, 279.

51. Maxine Greene, *Existential Encounters for Teachers* (New York: Random House, 1967), 4.

52. Greene, *Teacher as Stranger*, 255. For a further discussion on Sartre's concept of Anguish, see also Greene, *Dialectic of Freedom*, 5.

53. Sartre, *Being and Nothingness*, 489.

54. Sartre, *Being and Nothingness*, 66, in Marla Morris, *Existential and Phenomenological Influences on Maxine Greene*, 127.

55. Merleau-Ponty's methodology is dialectical because it stresses the internal and the relational connectedness of all things, and our analysis of the world must begin with relations. According to him there is no isolated sense datum in human perception, i.e., that the simplest element of perception is the gestalt structure of a figure on a background, a structure in which the elements define each other by their internal relations to each other. See Maurice Merleau-Ponty, *Phenomenology of Perception*, pp. 3–12.

Chapter Two

The Existential Concept of Freedom for Maxine Greene: The Influence of Freire and Merleau-Ponty on Greene's Educational Pedagogy

When freedom is the question, it is always time to begin.

—Maxine Greene[1]

The purpose of the preceding analysis of Sartre and Greene was to prepare the ground for, and inquire into, the moral usefulness of the work of these two thinkers to practical educators. As we saw in the previous chapter, Greene and Sartre both believe that it is through the dialectical principle of negativity and freedom that meaning and intelligibility are conferred upon the world in their manifest form. This notion is important throughout Greene's work, and is particularly important in *Dialectic of Freedom*, where Greene says about the student that "We must foster the freedom that he/she can attain as she moves dialectically between necessity and fulfillment, between the ineradicable qualities of her particular situation and the thus far unrealized capacities which are hers".[2]

Sartre's existentialist concept of freedom suggests that morality as a whole is the province of individual self-determination, and the social dimension of morality and relationships with others comes in simply as one element in the design of an individual life. Sartre's focus on individuality is particularly acute in *Being and Nothingness*. To use one's freedom of action, according to Sartre, means that one wills a world that bends to his or her desires. Rule-governed situations can be included within this world only to the extent that they can be shown to involve individual choice.

Greene, in emphasizing the social dimension of freedom, represents an advance on Sartre's individualistic philosophy. She is so faithful to the idea of an involved consciousness that the idea of a detached consciousness is largely negative in her cosmology of freedom. Greene believes that people are never alone but always stand in relation to others. In an interview, Greene drew attention to the importance of community: "I want young people to identify themselves by means of significant projects. It seems important as I have said too often that the projects are most meaningful when they involve others".[3] Moral education, according to Greene, must be specifically concerned with self-identification in a community.

In this chapter, I will examine how Greene further develops Sartre's concept of freedom by contextualizing it within an intersubjective realm. In emphasizing her development of Sartre's concept of freedom, this chapter will further elucidate the influence of Freire and Merleau-Ponty on Greene's work. The discussion will begin with an examination of Sartre's concept of ethics as it relates to freedom, as a critical evaluation of Sartre's thought may serve as the key to understanding both Greene's attempt to build upon Sartrean concepts and her redefinition of moral ethics. Human freedom for Greene, as for Sartre, manifests itself positively as grounded in possibility. But above and beyond her use of Sartre, I will go on to show how Greene interprets the concept of possibility within the intersubjective context of education. I will explore how the concept of freedom for Greene, as opposed to Sartre, is concretely rooted in a notion of multicultural literacy in which social equality and cultural differences coexist with the principles that inform substantive participatory democracy.

To this effect, I will first elucidate Paulo Freire's influence on Greene as it relates to naming and power structures within an educational setting. Both Freire and Greene suggest a view of empowerment in which learning becomes the basis for challenging social practices that produce symbolic and real violence. These practices render some students voiceless and thus stripped of their freedom, for acting, choosing, and naming are what make a person free.

The remainder of the chapter will show how Greene, by adopting Merleau-Ponty's concept of "social imagination," has created a successful educational pedagogy that recognizes the role of possibility, at the same time exploring the historical and social contexts of intersubjective relationships. Ultimately, in Chapter IV, I want to suggest that Greene moves beyond these philosophers by offering a literary pedagogy of imagination.

As Thomas Anderson, a renowned scholar of Sartre claims, throughout *Being and Nothingness*, Sartre seems to consider the choice of freedom to be primarily an individual one. He appears most interested in saying why free human beings do not choose their freedom but flee from it in pursuing a type of existence incompatible with it—namely by adopting the spirit of seriousness and living in bad faith. By "bad faith" Sartre designates the attempt by an individual to escape from what he or she is, to what he or she can never become.[4] The alternative he proposes is for an individual to undergo a "radical conversion" and to accept his or her freedom as his or her goal, as he believes that these considerations do not exclude the possibility of an ethics of deliverance and salvation. The description of the nature of this radical conversion was apparently left for his work on ethics, a work Sartre never completed.[5]

As Anderson points out later, in works such as *Saint Genet*[6] and *Critique of Dialectical Reason*,[7] Sartre did examine the situated character of human freedom, particularly with respect to the social dimension of many freedoms. Here he emphasizes the alienated state of human freedom in the world, its limitations, and the need for human cooperation to attain the goal of true freedom. But despite this emphasis on the social aspect of freedom, however, Sartre nowhere attempts to demonstrate systematically that the individual has a moral obligation to any freedom other than his own. In his discussions with de Beauvoir, Sartre noted the tension he felt between the requirements of freedom and the need for community, between his desire to safeguard his personal liberty and his need for others.[8] This is clear in the *Critique of Dialectical Reason*, where Sartre tries to set forth the structures of society and the various collectivities within it in their dialectical interrelations and in their relations to matter, an understanding of which would enable individuals more fully to control them instead of being controlled by them. But it is important to point out that the concept of group introduced by Sartre in the *Critique of Dialectical Reason* does not provide any room for a unity of consciousness. Instead, the praxis of group projects depends upon external forces, including threats and danger. Praxis involves all the individuals who make up the group; yet the individual project remains the core of the praxis, and the individual retains his or her central position as a free consciousness that can break away from the group even if punishment is inevitable. Thus, the shift from the individual-centered world of *Being and Nothingness* to the group-centered sociality of the *Critique of Dialectical Reason* is incomplete: it fails to resolve the conflict that marks the individual's relationship with the group as a whole.[9]

According to Anderson most commentators agree that in *Existentialism and Humanism* Sartre does refer to what he considers to be an individual's moral responsibility to others. Here he says, "I am obliged to will the freedom of others at the same time as mine. I cannot make freedom my aim unless I make that of others equally my aim".[10] However, Sartre's reasons for holding this view remain unclear. Why is one obliged to will not just one's personal freedom but also that of others? The suggestions Sartre makes in *Existentialism and Humanism* are inadequate. Sartre argues that all moral principles rest upon the individual's choice; therefore, there are no objective grounds for morality. If one accepts the relevance of a particular consideration, it is because one chooses to do so. There are no objective criteria to govern such choices. Nor does Sartre discuss in this regard the nature of the relation between authentic individuals. Rather, according to Sartre, each individual must simply choose his or her freedom, the continual expansion of his or her own existence[11].

Sartre's paradigm is thus one in which the individual, as moral agent, must choose and must act in isolation from or in the absence of a collectively accepted, mutual body of moral rules. As a result, critics have argued that Sartre's ethics legitimizes radical individualism, leading to chaos and anarchy. The "normal" situation, in which such guidance and support are available, receives relatively little attention from Sartre. Since action outside of reciprocal moral strictures is always threatened with "inauthenticity," it offers at best a marginal example of the "moral." Under this view, morality could in fact be equated with the whole province of human action, with no distinction made between the broader questions of individual self-determination and the questions that are usually seen as answered by reference not to an individual ideal but to a rule held as common by at least some subgroup.[12]

The other striking thing about Sartre's treatment of human relations in *Being and Nothingness* is the manner in which the author reasons out his position. According to Thomas Anderson, human relationships for Sartre are founded at an abstract level. Sartre not only refers to such relations as existing either between consciousnesses, or in and of themselves, rather than between human beings, he sees these relationships as occurring almost exclusively on the psychological level.[13] When Sartre writes, for example, of a subject being alienated, degraded, or enslaved by another, this slavery is only psychological. Similarly, rather than addressing human beings, Sartre refers to consciousness coming to self-awareness by negating, even wrenching away from, the other. Through this process, consciousness recognizes that it is not the reified object the other makes of it but a free subject.[14] Again, the recognition of one's freedom does not necessarily involve any concrete social and political liberation from the other; the fact that the slave can freely choose the meaning of his slavery does not free him or her from the limitations and restrictions of slavery, and this includes those it places on his or her choice.[15]

Likewise, for Sartre, deliverance from conflict comes, when possible at all, not from real physical actions or from reforming oppressive political and socioeconomic structures, but from changing consciousness. Thus, the radical conversion Sartre briefly alluded to consists of a fundamental change in an individual's choices that arises out of an individual mental response to the concrete social problems of human relations. Though this remedy may be ethical,

it is fundamentally apolitical and ahistorical.[16] Anderson emphasizes this
point in the following passage:

> I simply wish to stress that it is only this kind of degradation that Sartre consid-
> ers in these pages devoted to human relationships. To repeat, his discussion of
> the impact of others on one's freedom examines human beings and their rela-
> tions only insofar as they involve consciousness' objectification of one subject
> by another, and a subject's free conferral of meaning on that objectification, not
> insofar as they involve real physical, political, or economic actions or structures
> which enhance or deform human existence. In other words, it is basically rela-
> tions between consciousnesses that Sartre discusses, not concrete relations be-
> tween flesh and blood human beings immersed in history and in its sociopoliti-
> cal systems.[17]

Thus, Sartre has at best shown that an individual should choose to value his
condition as a being free by nature and able to choose freely within real situations. He has not, however, demonstrated why any individual needs to increase
or concretize this free choice by modifying the situation in order to increase
his or her available options.[18]

As Anderson notes, it is only fair to point out that Sartre is not simply attempting to present a laissez-faire approach to morality. Sartre's existentialist
ethics address the issue of individuals who are required to act in circumstances in which the support "normally" expected from established moral institutions is for some reason unavailable. Moreover, even when the choice is
made in the context of a functioning society to which the moral agent be-
longs, Sartre usually describes a context that undermines the assumption of a
moral consensus or of any genuine reciprocity.[19]

It is important to point out that given there is a difference between metaphysical or transcendental freedom on the one hand (free will) and empirical
or social freedom on the other (emancipation). Sartre, following Immanuel
Kant believes that the former has normative implications for the latter, that is,
that the very fact that we are free beings implies that some ways of treating
people are wrong, some are right. But Sartre never works this out, not least of
all because he rejects Kant's own moral theory: that freedom means autonomy, that autonomy means rational self-legislation, which in turn demands
adherence to the moral law in the form of the categorical imperative, etc.
Thus individuals for Sartre are ultimately are morally responsible only for
themselves.

Elaborating on Sartre's concept of choice, Greene believes that individuals
always define their freedom in relation with others. Although it is equally important for her to affirm that the decision is always the act of an individual
acting voluntarily in a particular situation at a particular moment, she does not

believe that individuals are isolated, answerable only to themselves. As Greene explicitly states: "I do mean that individuals, viewed as participants, as inextricably involved with other people, must be enabled to take responsibility for their own choosing".[20] The aim for her is to find an authentic public space, one in which diverse human beings can appear before one another. Such a space requires the provision of opportunities for the articulation of multiple perspectives in multiple idioms, out of which something common can be brought into being. With this in mind, Greene wants to explore other ways of seeing, alternate modes of being in the world.

In *Dialectic of Freedom*, Greene maintains that it is "through and by means of education . . . that individuals can be provoked to reach beyond themselves in their intersubjective space. It is through and by means of education that they may become empowered to think about what they are doing".[21] And fundamental to this whole process of learning, Greene states:

> is the sense of moral directedness, of oughtness. An imaginativeness, an awareness and a sense of possibility are required, along with the sense of autonomy and agency, of being present to the self. . . . As wide awake teachers work, making principles available and eliciting moral judgments, they must orient themselves to the concrete, the relevant, and the questionable.[22]

Education, according to Greene, is conceived as "a process of futuring, of releasing persons to become different and to take actions to create themselves".[23] The challenge for Greene is to engage as many young people as possible, thus motivating them toward what she calls "collective action."[24] Emphasizing the connection between education and freedom, Greene reinforces the themes of decision and choosing, as she stated in her inaugural lecture as William F. Russell Professor of Education at Teachers College, Columbia University in 1975: "My concern is [with] what can be done by means of education to enable people to transcend their private terrors and act together to give freedom a concrete existence in their lives".[25] And, further separating herself from Sartre, she goes on to say, "My interest is not so much freedom from or negative freedom as it is the deliberate creation of the kinds of conditions in which people can be themselves".[26]

Moral sensitivity for Greene, in contrast to Sartre, is a crucial aspect of a student's learning. As she states in *The Landscapes of Learning*,

> If teachers today are to initiate young people into an ethical existence, they themselves must attend more fully than they normally have to their own lives . . . , they have to break with the mechanical life, to overcome their own submergence in the habitual, even in what they conceive to be virtuous, and ask the 'why' in which learning and moral reasoning begin.[27]

Greene in turn believes that the young "are most likely to be stirred to learn when they are challenged by teachers who themselves are learning, who are breaking with what they have too easily taken for granted, who are creating their own moral lives".[28] And further: "if educators, whoever we are, can become challengers to impersonality . . . , challengers to suffering and [to] lack of care, if we take initiatives, we can begin to recreate an educational space in which meanings can emerge for persons as they take the risk of risking and begin choosing the moral life and in the process define their freedom".[29]

It is important to note that, for Greene, students are unlikely to articulate their perspectives or to pose questions about their social reality if they are not enabled to reflect on their own consciousnesses. To this effect, she encourages self-reflection. It is important for her that teachers and teacher educators also be stimulated to think about their own thinking and to reflect upon their own reflecting. This leads to "inherently liberating" thinking and is likely to invigorate both their teaching and their advocacy.[30] By helping students make sense of their world, education, according to Greene, serves what Paulo Freire calls a "liberatory function,"[31] a function that is inherently intersubjective and social. Greene makes Freire's existentialist concept of vocation her primary aim in *The Dialectic of Freedom:*

> it is not difficult to be reminded of Paulo Freire writing of humanization as our primary vocation—the struggle for the overcoming of alienation, for the affirmation of men and women as persons. It is with a similar vocation and situatedness that I speak of the 'dialectic of freedom.'[32]

Influenced by Freire's critical pedagogy, Greene's educational pedagogy assumes that the teacher's efforts aim always to bring the student from one state of being to another state of being. They bring about an observable progress in the behaviors of the student.

Like Greene, Freire is an educator who treats knowing in a critical and self-reflective fashion and refuses to take the social and cultural matrix as a given. As Greene herself puts it in *Landscapes of Learning,* "according to Freire men engage in praxis when their action encompasses a critical reflection which increasingly organizes their thinking and thus leads them to move from a purely naive knowledge of reality to a higher level, one which enables them to perceive the cause of reality".[33] In other words, in naming their world, individuals pose relevant questions and pursue answers with a sense of reality to be produced and with the intention of bringing about a projected state of affairs.

In *Pedagogy of the Oppressed*, Freire stresses the central role of dialogue in a pedagogy that would build conscience. Dialogue, for Freire, requires teachers to submerge their egos and engage trustfully with their students in discourse on oppression. In the absence of dialogue, Freire believes, communication cannot take place; and without communication, there can be no education. Political education humanizes by its very nature, and pedagogy must therefore permit the emergence of the student's humanization from the start.[34] Freire defines dialogue as the encounter between individuals, mediated by the world, in order to name the world. The only domination allowed in this process is that of the world by the dialoguer. This, says Freire, "is the conquest of the world for the liberation of men".[35]

At the center of Freire's whole argument are two basic concepts—the word and the act of naming. Human existence cannot be silent, nor can it be nourished by false words, but only by true words with which individuals transform the world. To exist humanely for Freire "is to name the world, to change it. Once named the world in turn reappears to the namers as a problem and requires of them a new *naming*".[36] Freire asserts that the fundamental nature of language is vocal. Human beings, he believes, "are not built in silence but in word, in work, in action".[37] The linguistic activity that involves the act of naming and the use of the word thus focuses on the world. All this is directed toward the humanization of the individual.

For Freire, as for many thinkers, naming is an act of creation. For the oppressed to rise to a level of critical consciousness entails the falling away of the oppressors' universe of words. But the recovery of language as authentic intentionality also requires the liberation of the primary senses, the very tools of perception.[38] In dialogue, people set out to name the world, that is, to realign and reinvent relationships between word and object, or to distinguish the word that conceals from the word that reveals.

Greene clearly aligns herself with Freire in agreeing that dialogue is in itself a process of humanization. Dialogue permits students to express their own intentionality about the world, and this is one way that Greene suggests educators can begin to create a new pedagogy. The "subversive" effects of dialogue in teaching, according to Greene, are limitless. With situations opened via teaching, students may become empowered to engage in some sort of praxis, may become engaged enough to name the obstacles to their shared becoming.[39] Once students begin to name the world, they transform through their own actions their individual lives.

Greene holds that an inability to articulate interferes with the processes of education and learning. Insofar as students are submerged in the voices of power that control them, they are unable to critically reinterpret their surroundings. As Greene says:

> If diverse human voices can become more and more audible, if more and more publics can be formed and become articulate, the mystifying languages will become in some manner transparent. We will hear the sounds of desire as we open

subversive→subvert : to destroy completely; ruin, to overthrow
ok - that's what I thought it meant — so, to name & overcome
through dialogue

ourselves to more and more stories, and we will hear articulations of new visions and possibilities open as people begin to recognize the incompleteness of things if the sense of possibility is really to be enhanced.[40]

It is through the process of naming that the awareness of one's freedom is finally achieved. According to Greene, by naming the obstacles that stand in their way, human beings act on their desire to reach toward wider spaces for fulfillment, to expand options, to know alternatives.[41] A space is opened up for them that makes authentic dialogue possible:

> The stuff of life seems formless and blank to those who are in Paulo Freire's sense 'oppressed,' who have to be aroused to a consciousness of how the real is constructed and who have to be challenged to name their lived world, and through the naming, to transform those worlds.[42]

The underlying assumption of Greene's pedagogy is that human beings are beings in the world and are always in the process of constructing themselves by turning from their actualities to their potentialities; these potentialities are in turn discovered in relationship with others. As she says in *Dialectic of Freedom*, "the world should be filled with meaning of students' existential experience and not of their teachers. Our role as teachers and teacher educators is to encourage and provoke students to speak in their own voice in a world where other voices define the mainstream".[43]

For Greene, the growth of a new critical awareness is a rediscovery of the familiar, from which emerges a fresh use of old words. If the senses are set free, and begin to see what *is* rather than what the world of domination compelled them to see, the liberated person needs a new idiom in which to name what is seen for the first time. The goal, for her, is to recognize that in this world of multiple viewpoints no reckoning, whether that of the pedagogue or of another, can ever be finished or complete. There is always a possibility for different views, experiences, and ways of being in the world. As she says, "it is within this possibility that space opens for the pursuit of freedom within a public space,"[44] where persons appear before one another as who they really are and what they really can do.

Greene's preoccupation with the diversity and particularity of American voices has led her over time to an interest in the notion of multiple perspectives and in Hannah Arendt's vision of a public space that leads to a pedagogy of empowerment, a kind of pedagogy oriented to the enlargement and enrichment of perspectives through involvement with multiple ways of knowing, multiple disciplines, and multiple forms of life. Greene's reading of Arendt's *The Human Condition*[45] thus focuses on how the latter conceptualizes the existence of public space.[46] Within the context of education, the aim for Greene, is to find how situations can be created in which persons consciously choose to appear before one another in the open, to come together in speech and action, as the best as they know how to be.[47]

According to Greene, Arendt sees crucial connections between power, freedom and the public space. Freedom, for Arendt, is located in the public realm, and the backbone of this freedom is "human reality," conceived as "the basic condition of both action and speech".[48] Action and speech, we recall, are power; and freedom is "identified with a space that provide[s] room for human action and interaction".[49] Greene believes that the space in question ought to be one infused with an imaginative awareness, to allow those involved to imagine alternative possibilities for their own becoming.[50] It has to be a space in which individuals mutually discover, recognize and appreciate alternate ways of conceiving realities, consequently finding ways to make sense of their intersubjective world.

Greene, by invoking the phenomenologist Merleau-Ponty's concept of social imagination (which she defines as the capacity to invent visions of what should be and what ought to be),[51] shows that the world we inhabit is the interpersonal world of human coexistence. Phenomenology which examines the structures of human experience, is a philosophy which considers the comprehension of human beings and the world impossible from any other basis than the facticity of existence. According to Merleau-Ponty, human beings are essentially historical beings whose identity, unity, and autonomy as individual selves are always in a dialectical process of developing. Their identities are thus part of an ongoing history of human imaginative responses to situations whose inherent ambiguity and mystifying power involve us in a continual struggle to always be more than we are already: "The world," Merleau-Ponty therefore writes, "is not what I think but what I live through".[52] And it is in the very inexhaustibility of the world, Greene suggests, "that the search for ways of articulation or sense making will be ongoing".[53]

Imagination, for Greene, gives rise to glimpses of possibility, to what is not yet, to what ought to be. Any encounter, she says,

> with the actual human beings who are trying to learn how to learn requires imagination on the part of teachers and on the part of those they teach . . . .[I]t takes imagination to become aware that a search is possible . . . .[I]t takes imagination on the part of the young people to perceive openings through which they can move.[54]

Greene believes that imagination is as important in the lives of teachers as it is in the lives of their students, in part, she says, because teachers incapable of thinking imaginatively or of releasing students to encounter works of literature and other forms of art are probably also unable to communicate to the young what the use of imagination signifies. If it is the case that imagination feeds one's capacity to feel one's way into another's vantage point, then teachers may also be lacking in empathy.[55]

Consequently, one of the reasons Greene says she comes

to concentrate on imagination as a means though which we can assemble a coherent world is that imagination is that, above all, which makes empathy possible. As it helps give credence to alternative realities, it allows us to break with the taken for granted and set aside familiar distinctions and definitions.[56]

Drawing on Merleau-Ponty's concept of embodied consciousness, in which perception undergirds cognition, Greene identifies consciousness as something experienced through the movements and gestures that embody us in space, time and history, our differentiation from and integration with our past, with other human beings and with the world in which we move about and live.[57] For Merleau-Ponty the dialectical concept of experience is contextualized within the lived perception of the individual subject, at the same time immediately opening to a world beyond the subject; because he believes that a fundamental element of a subject's perception is its perspectival character. It is partial and incomplete and presented in a way that possibility of other perspectives are always open. So instead of starting with a specific individual's experience and connecting his or her projects with the projects of other individuals, as Sartre does, Merleau-Ponty argues that as soon as I perceive the world, I am immediately in a world with others.[58] He argues that the very first things perceived in the nascent perception are other human beings, a belief that arises out of a dialectical relationship between consciousness and the body and between an individual and its relationship to other individuals, a view contrary to what Sartre has put forth. The meaning of the human world he says is: "the recognition beyond the present milieu of a world of things visible for each "I" under a plurality of aspects, the taking of indefinite time and space."[59]

Similarly, Greene stresses that perception is embodied, and that: "we are first cast into the world as embodied beings".[60] Through the language we speak, we are, Greene says, embodied in social roles, in cultures and subcultures, in forms of thinking, of understanding and of imagining. By attending, listening, and gazing, Greene maintains, a perceiver structures what presents itself. She goes on to say:

As Merleau-Ponty puts it, perceiving entails a return to the 'there is' underlying an abstract conception, to the 'object-in-general' or to the site, the soil of the sensible and the opened world such as it is in our life and body (M. Merleau-

nascent - coming into existence; emerging, to be born

Ponty, *The Primacy of Perception* (1964, Evanston, IL: Northwestern University Press) p. 160). The way things are allows us only a partial view of things, not the kind of total view we might gain if we were godlike, looking down from the sky. But we can only know as situated beings. We see aspects of objects and people around us; we all live in the kind of incompleteness that Freire identified, and there is always more for us to see.[61]

Consequently, the situations in which choices concerning one's freedom take place are always embodied and socialized. The way in which the individual addresses himself or herself to the process of attending, judging, and choosing will be affected to the degree he or she is with others, the degree to which they have experienced the "we relation" in the world. Such relations are then, by virtue of their intersubjectivity, moral decisions. In a related quote Greene says a human being:

> lives as it were in two orders—one created by his or her relations with the perceptual fields that are given in experience, the other created by his or her relations with a human and social environment. It is important to remember that each of us achieves contact with the world from a particular vantage point, in terms of a partial biography. All this underlies our present perspectives and affects the way we look at things and structure our realities. To be in touch with our landscape is to be conscious of our evolving experiences, to be aware of the ways in which we encounter the world.[62]

For both Merleau-Ponty and Greene, freedom and morality are commensurable and rooted in the world of which the other, another human being, is the predominant reality. Existence in this context is not "condemned to freedom" as it is for Sartre, but judged and invested as freedom. An important implication of this is that one is not an agent "over against" society. Rather than others being a threat to one's agency, as was the case for Sartre, others are the occasion for possibility. Humans as agents, then, are intimately connected with others. As Greene states:

> To articulate norms and principles to those prepared to hear, to make them visible to those who participated in shared activities, is to encourage the taking of responsibility by such individuals, whoever they may be. Autonomy signifies the conviction of moral responsibility, as it involves sense of personal agency. When human beings feel submerged and channeled, it is difficult for them to be self determining. We must understand that the enlightenment heritage must be repossessed and reinterpreted so that we can overcome the positivism that awaits us on one side and the empty universalism on the other. But we cannot and ought not to escape our memories, our histories, not if we are to keep alive the awareness that grounds our identities and connects us to the persons turning for fulfillment in our actions.[63]

According to Greene, moral choice, in the context of Merleau-Ponty's notion of embodied perception, requires choosing between two alternatives, typ-
ically between two goods. The task of the educator is to empower students to
internalize principles that will enable them to make such choices. These, says
Greene, "are choices of consequence for the self and others, and they are
made and can only be made in social situations where custom, tradition, offi-
cial codes, and laws condition and play upon what people think and do".[64]

In conclusion, this chapter has tried to show how Greene, by further developing Sartre's concept of freedom to include the educational and the intersubjective realm, creates an educational pedagogy where human beings
perceive the world as always situated. And the situated person as Greene says:
"inevitably engaged with others, reaches out and grasps the phenomena surrounding him/her from a particular vantage point and against a particular
background of consciousness."[65] Freedom then becomes not only a matter of
being, it becomes our experience in an embodied way.

But embodied freedom within such a context for Greene must be critical
and self-reflective, a demand that people ponder what they imagine, that they
articulate the principles that govern the choices they make as they live. What,
after all, Greene asks, "is the relationship between imagination and moral
life?"[66] She goes on to answer herself:

> I try to connect it, for example, to a kind of face to face morality—the morality
> that finds expression in coming towards another person, looking . . . him or her
> in the eyes, gazing not simply glancing . . . it is a matter of affirming. . . . [O]ne
> person is there for the other, looking him/her in the face, answering the social
> demand . . . .[S]ocial imagination involves looking at the world as if it could
> be otherwise.[67]

Greene locates the condition for such a possibility in the realm of literature.
Works of literature, according to Greene, allow the imaginative mode of apprehension to break with the stereotyped, the conventional, and the mundane. They
empower the individual to explore his or her inner horizons, to reflect upon his
or her own consciousness and capacity for knowing. To be "literate" in this fashion, for Greene, is to be able to crack the codes that have kept secret so many visions of freedom and fulfillment, to allow the existence of created worlds.[68]

To appeal to the freedom of the individual, to enable students to confront
their own reality, imaginative art should, according to Greene, always be offered as present possibilities—as beginnings rather than culminations, as ori-
gins, rather than means or ends.[69] And when such an imaginative dialogue is
activated in classrooms, even the young are stirred to reach out on their own
initiatives.[70] The next chapter will deal with the relevance of interpreting literary texts within the context of Greene's curriculum of freedom.

*This chapter has been adapted from Shaireen Rasheed, "The Existential Concept of Freedom for Maxine Greene: The Influence of Sartre and Merleau-Ponty on Greene's Educational Pedagogy," in Philosophy of Education 2002, ed. Scott Fletcher (Urbana, Illinois: Philosophy of Education Society, 2003), 394–401. Reprinted by permission of Philosophy of Education Society.

NOTES

1. Maxine Greene, *Dialectic of Freedom*,(New York: Teachers College Press, 1988) 155.

2. Ibid., 163.

3. W. Ayers, "Interview with Maxine Greene," *Qualitative Studies in Education* 8/4 (1995): 319.

4. Thomas Anderson, *The Structure and Foundation of Sartrean Ethics*. Kansas: Regents Press, 1979. pp. 67–68. See also Sartre, *Being and Nothingness*, trans. Hazel E. Barnes. (New York: Philosophical Library 1956) part 1, chapter 2. For a related discussion see Richard J. Bernstein, *Praxis and Action* (Philadelphia: University of Pennsylvania Press, 1971, 149; see also 148–152.

5. Ibid. See also *Being and Nothingness*, 312, also n. 14

6. Jean-Paul Sartre, *Saint Genet: Actor and Martyr*, trans. B. Frechtman (New York: New American Library, Mentor Books, 1963).

7. Jean-Paul Sartre, *Critique of Dialectical Reason*, trans. Alan Sheridan-Smith (London: NLB, 1976).

8. Anderson, *The Structure and Foundation of Sartrean Ethics*, p.68. See also Simone de Beauvoir, *Force of Circumstance*, trans. Richard Howard (New York: G.P. Putnam's Sons, 1964), especially 243, 261.

9. See Khemais Benhamida, "Sartre's Existentialism and Education: The Missing Foundation of Human Relations." *Educational Theory* 23/3 (Summer 1973) 235.

10. Jean-Paul Sartre, *Existentialism and Humanism* Transl. P. Mairet (London: Methuen Ltd., 1973), 52.

11. Anderson, *The Structure and Foundation of Sartrean Ethics*, p.68

12. See Frederick A. Olafson, "Authenticity and Obligation," in *Sartre: A Collection of Critical Essays*, ed. Mary Warnock, (Garden City: Anchor Books, 1971), 123.

13. Thomas C. Anderson, *Sartre's Two Ethics: From Authenticity to Integral Humanity* (Illinois: Open Court, 1993), 27.

14. Ibid., 30.

15. Ibid.

16. Ibid., 35.

17. Ibid., 31.

18. Ibid., 55.

19. Ibid., 65–67.

20. Maxine Greene, *Landscapes of Learning* (New York: Teachers College Press, 1978), 2.

21. Greene, *Dialectic of Freedom*, 12.

22. Greene, *Landscapes of Learning*, 51.

23. Greene, *Dialectic of Freedom*, 22.

24. Ibid., 125.

25. Maxine Greene, *Education, Freedom and Possibility* (Inaugural Lecture as William F. Russell Professor) (New York: Teachers College, Columbia University, 1975).

26. Ibid. p.

27. Greene, *Landscapes of Learning*, 46.

28. Ibid., 51.

29. Ibid., 157.

30. Ibid., 61.

31. Maxine Greene, *Teacher as Stranger: Educational Philosophy for the Modern Age* (Belmont, Calif.: Wadsworth Publishing Company, 1973), 163.

32. Greene, *Dialectic of Freedom*, 8.

33. Greene, *Landscapes of Learning*, 163.

34. According to Freire, dialogue is in itself a process of humanization. For dialogue permits students to express their own intentionality about the world. As Freire says, "dialogue is the encounter between men, mediated by the world in order to name the world." Paulo Freire, *Pedagogy of the Oppressed*, trans. Myra Bergman Ramos (New York: Continuum Publishing Company), 69.

35. Freire, *Pedagogy of the Oppressed*, pp. 76–7.

36. Ibid.

37. Ibid.

38. See Toby Tafirenyika Moyana, *Education Liberation and the Creative Act* (Harare, Zimbabwe: Zimbabwe Publishing House, 1988), 29.

39. Greene, *Dialectic of Freedom*, 133.

40. Ibid., 132.

41. Ibid., 5.

42. Maxine Greene, *Releasing the Imagination: Essays on Education, the Arts, and Social Change* (San Francisco: Jossey-Bass Inc., 1995), 24.

43. Greene, *Dialectic of Freedom*, 190.

44. Greene, *Dialectic of Freedom*, 128.

45. Hannah Arendt, *The Human Condition* (Chicago: Chicago University Press, 1958).

46. For an in depth discussion on this topic see Norm Fruchter, "Pursuing Public Space: Maxine Greene and Sameness in Utter Diversity," in *A Light in Dark Time: Maxine Greene and the Unfinished Conversation*, eds. William Ayers and Janet L. Miller (New York: Teachers College Press, 1998), 229.

47. Maxine Greene, "Public Spaces in Local Places," *Phenomenology and Pedagogy* 10 (1992): 245.

48. See Greene, *Dialectic of Freedom*, 116.

49. Ibid., 120.

50. Greene, *Releasing the Imagination*, 39.

51. Ibid., 5.

52. Maurice Merleau-Ponty, *Phenomenology of Perception* (London: Routledge and Kegan Paul, 1967), xvi-xvii. According to Merleau-Ponty the logic of the world is a "living cohesion" in which I belong to myself while belonging to the world. Merleau-Ponty's conception of phenomenology is rooted in a philosophy of the embodied world and nature, an aspect he was still working on in the Visible and the Invisible, when he died. *The Visible and the Invisible*, followed by Working Notes, ed. Claude Lefort, trans. Alphonso Lingis (Evanston, Ill.: Northwestern University Press, 1968).

53. Greene, *Releasing the Imagination*, 107.

54. Ibid., 14.

55. Ibid., 36.

56. Ibid., 3.

57. *The Phenomenology of Perception* explicitly deals with this process in its examination of perception and the world. In an overcoming of this duality of mind/consciousness over world, perception for Merleau-Ponty is the primary function of the human organism and of the human body, constituting the only adequate foundation for a theory of perception. See M.C. Dillon, *Merleau-Ponty's Ontology* (Indianapolis: Indiana University Press, 1998), 105.

58. The phenomenal body as he claims then, "is the vantage point from which I perceive all possible objects. It is my body which is the vehicle of my perception and movement in the world." Merleau-Ponty, *Phenomenology of Perception*, 111

59. The underlying aim for him being one of teaching individual to see and to learn what perceptions mean against our falsification that our mental constructs impose. It requires that we must learn what we have already taken the trouble to learn, called radical reflection, "reflection on the unreflected, it appeals to a conception of the a priori synthetic which no longer sets the a priori off against the factual but integrates the a priori with the factual, shows that the incompleteness of actual precepts is a necessary feature of the perceptual praxis." Christopher Macann, *Four Phenomenological Philosophers: Husserl, Heidegger, Sartre and Merleau-Ponty* (London: Routledge 1993) pp. 182, 171

60. Greene, *Releasing the Imagination*, 73.

61. Ibid., 26.

62. Greene, *Landscapes of Learning*, 2.

63. Ibid., 6.

64. Ibid., 48.

65. Greene, *Dialectic of Freedom*, 21

66. W. Ayers, "Interview with Maxine Greene," *Qualitative Studies in Education* 8/4 (1995): 319328.

67. Ibid.

68. See Maxine Greene, "Literature, Existentialism and Education, in, ed. David E. Dentons (New York: Teachers College Press, 1974), 84.

69. See Ibid., 80–83.

70. Ibid.

Chapter Three

A Pedagogy of Pluralism:
The Literary Reality of Lived Worlds

Accessibility, which is a process, is often taken for a natural, self-evident state of language. What is perpetuated in its name is a given form of intolerance and an unacknowledged practice of exclusion. Thus, as long as the complexity and difficulty of engaging with the diversely hybrid experiences of heterogeneous contemporary societies are denied and not dealt with, binary thinking continues to mark time while the creative interval is dangerously reduced to non-existence.[1] *binary - 2 parts/components*

For Maxine Greene, critical pedagogy is not a standardized methodology but a process that accounts both for social, political, and historical conditions and for the perspectives and considerations of the participants of a given moment. In her words, "because the problems of education are profound and [because] educators' notions of the possibilities for change are limited by this constrained discourse of standardization, it is often difficult even to envision more humane, more just, and more democratic alternatives".[2] Few educators today, Greene states:

> can escape the impact of cultural diversity or the sounds of newly audible 'voices' seldom attended to before. The implications for our conceptions of curriculum content are considerable. Questions are raised about the American tradition, about the American Dream, about what can and should be transmitted to the changing populations in our schools. In addition, with a growing awareness of multiple meanings in the various areas of study, teachers and administrators are beginning to seek out alternative ways of representing what is known and what the young are expected to respect and understand. Educators who have not been exposed to the nuances of changing approaches to the history of ideas and the history of the schools are unlikely to respond well to the challenges that increasing diversity now poses for them.[3]

heterogeneous - consisting of dissimilar elements/parts

40

By incorporating literature that reflects students' lives, she believes education can begin to create a pedagogy that, working through and beyond the confines of modernist thought, is relevant and meaningful to the multiple experiences and realities that students face. Throughout her numerous works, Greene illustrates what philosophy and education can learn from literature, which is precisely the business of catering to images of human dignity.

In this chapter, I will elucidate how Greene, by incorporating literature into her work, seeks to move her readers to critical and more self-reflective practice. I will go on to explain how such an encompassing theory of education creates a space in which possibility and freedom exist simultaneously.

In *What is Literature*, Sartre reminds us that every reader and writer presents a world he or she has in common with his or her readers, a world that the writer explores and examines with his freedom. Sartre goes on to say that literature is not meant to entertain or amuse us. Its function is to convert. The writer discloses the world in order to change it. This is the meaning of the popular term *literature engage:* "the author has given up the impossible dream of giving an impartial picture of society and the human condition"[4] This is why Sartre's novels do not present a single word or a single attitude. As the historical situation changes, there are corresponding changes in the stance to be taken.

The world of Sartre's novels, according to Greene, is a "rectification" of the world in which the reader lives, and so Sartre's novels satisfy a metaphysical need. But if literature is to constitute a significant rebellion, it must, according to Sartre, reveal itself to the indignation of the reader, an indignation that holds within it a promise to change. To change does not mean to alter sensibility or expectation; it means to transcend, to refuse, and to realize, to move towards what does not yet exist.[5]

According to Greene, the author of a novel, for Sartre,

> sets up landmarks for the readers, but the landmarks are 'separated by the void'; it is up to the reader to unite them, to go beyond them and create a whole. An engagement with literature becomes therefore paradigmatic; it involves self- ~~show/see~~ transcendence and the creation of orders, even as it enables us to look, by dint of imagination, upon the great metaphysical constants like birth, death, seeking, relationship—and to return to things themselves.[6]

Like Sartre, Greene uses literature to describe the human condition. Influenced by Sartre's artistic use of literature, she in turn uses literary texts to elucidate an existentialist relationship of human beings with their surroundings. According to Greene, if literature can arouse individuals to reflective consciousness, it can arouse them to an awareness of new possibilities, new openings; it may even move them to act upon the freedom that has been addressed.

Similar to Sartre's claim, Greene holds that the reader, as entrant into a created world who seeks to disclose to him or herself a world of value, cannot allow the imagination to be limited to one-dimensional seeing. If we open ourselves rather as imaginative, intuitive, sensitive, intellectual beings, we may discover what it is to create our own meanings intersubjectively with other human creatures. Thus, through literature, we can recognize openings in situations, and these openings make possible the kind of action or transcendence that allows the individual to go beyond what he or she has been. In "Literature, Existentialism and Education," She goes on to say that, "since consciousness is intentional, always consciousness of something, the book presents a pre reality, or an aspect of the historical situation in which the writer lives his life".[7]

But as the previous chapter suggests, Greene differs from Sartre in her commitment to creating an educational pedagogy. For Greene, to educate is to take seriously both the quest for life's meaning and the meaning of individual lives. Through our accounts of the use of stories and personal narratives in educational practice, we can explore the centrality of narrative to the kind of work that teachers and counselors do. Those engaged in the work of telling, writing, reading, and listening to life stories can pass through cultural barriers to discover the power of the self and the integrity of the other. In doing so, they can expand their comprehension of their own histories and possibilities.

There is a need, according to Greene, to attend to the subject matter in expanding the range and content of communication and the possibility of finding emancipatory interest in what we think of as the disciplines. As Greene explicitly states, "the disciplines, the organized knowledge structures, ought to be offered as possibilities to individual participants, each with the capacity to generate structures that relate to his or her concerns, that clarify what he or she wants to say".[8] Greene does this by incorporating and emphasizing the uses of literary and other aesthetic experiences in stimulating the kinds of reflectiveness necessary for the pedagogy most of us wish to see.

Literature, for Greene, is a process of narratives opening up new possibilities. Greene's goal is to enrich and complement discursive accounts of classroom practice with works that involve readers not only with visions of the possible, but also with awareness of the contradictions and of the incompleteness that engage human beings in significant questions about their work and their world. These discourses involve us as historical beings born into a social reality. As individuals experience a work of literature through and by means of their own lived worlds, the realities they discover, according to Greene, "may well provide new vantage points on the inter subjective world, the world they share with others, the enrichment of the I, [leading to] an overcoming of silence and a quest for tomorrow, for what is not yet"[9]

discursive – covering a wide field of subjects

In a mode of personal reflection, Greene exemplifies this view with an autobiographical story of possibility in which she explores the world of literature. Stories, she says, are what made her see alternate realities. It was through stories that she learned about "uncertainties," learned to go beyond simply putting up with the ambiguities that were a part of her world. She learned, instead, to take these ambiguities or conflicts and work them over in her mind in a deliberate struggle to find meaning. Through story, Greene learned to understand ideas and to link them up to her own lived world of experiences. Through narratives, she came to understand the "autobiographical digging" that took place each time she remembered and reconstructed her experiences—through a new story process. As she explains:

learning + growing w/out actually having to go thru experience -visiting + learning thru someone else's eye

Through story I learnt about uncertainty, and I learnt to do more than just tolerate the ambiguities that seemed so much part of my world, I learnt to take up those ambiguities or conflicts and work them over and over in my mind to find meaning, through story I came to understand ideas that were often abstract by connecting those ideas to my own lived experience. Through stories dignifying my mother's and father's experiences I came to appreciate [the] value of narrative—including books and other forms of aesthetic material. And I especially grew to understand that the kind of autobiographical digging that took place each time they remembered and reconstructed their experiences through story was not only valuable for them but also for me. Their practice had created in me the habit of imagining, digging deep, of remembering, of listening to stories, of assessing, of reconstructing, of questioning a particular construction and of reconstructing again.[10]

What Greene attempts to do through literature is to blend personal narratives with public information, in order both to deconstruct boundaries and to create spaces. Spaces create space for desire, along with which arise hope and expectation. Poems and novels and stories often address our freedom, invite us to move beyond where we are, to move beyond ourselves. Reading these works within the context of schools and education, students will begin to ask questions, pose problems, and think beyond and between the boundaries by which they are defined. Consequently, the purpose of art within the context of imagination becomes for Greene one that reflects a sense of possibility, creating spaces in which freedom can exist. Imaginative literature, according to Greene, has the capacity to "awaken human beings to their condition, to make [them] aware of their awareness, present to themselves".[11] It is thus the most likely medium for releasing our students' imaginative capacities.

Using literature as a mode of education, according to Greene, creates spaces for students to question their preoccupation with human freedom and human growth. As a result, she says, we may "awaken others to possibility

opportunity to see beyond your own backyard

attenuate — to make slender; reduce, weaken, lessen

literature — free the weak, awaken the self, the "I"

and [to] the need for action in the name of possibility".[12] But a major theoretical issue this poses is how to approach literature and reading in terms of cultural diversity and of the structure of the curriculum. Greene, for her part, argues against conventional wisdom and proposes aesthetic encounters that are bound to disturb if they do not simply confuse. She requires that educators pay attention to a specific kind of literature:

> I am asking that attention be paid to a certain literature that seems on the face of it irrelevant to teacher education, a literature whose critical elements have been effectively absorbed. The reason is, again, that literature may have an emancipatory function for people whose selves have been attenuated, who have forgotten the function of the 'I'. I do not see how individuals who know nothing about the 'powers of darkness,' who account for themselves by talking about 'chance, circumstances and the times,' can awaken the young to question and learn.[13]

This implies that to celebrate world cultures it is not sufficient to teach courses or units on these cultures or to treat the texts as if the writer did not exist or as if the reader could examine only his or her own response to the text. We must instead unmask ignorance in the teaching of literature. There can be no expectation that the naive readers will comprehend cultural differences so long as all texts are treated as contemporary, genderless, and mainstream. Anonymity, in other words, is a dangerous fallacy. To see literature, ourselves, and our cultural whole, it is necessary to view texts as the works of real human beings, beings with both a past and a culture of their own.

An example of such a specific literary moral imperative is given by Nel Noddings in her essay "Ethics and Imagination."[14] In this essay, Noddings discusses the role of the arts, especially literature, in the teaching of ethics in an effort to develop ethical imagination and motivation in students. To further illustrate her point, she uses the example of *Uncle Tom's Cabin*:

> Consider *Uncle Tom's Cabin*. At the time Stowe wrote her novel, debate raged over the rightness and wrongness of slavery. A conversation between two of Stowe's characters illustrates the difference between a rational-feeling approach and a rational approach that has escaped the domain of feeling entirely. Mrs. Shelby reacts with horror to her husband's decision to sell Uncle Tom and little Harry. Her husband argues financial necessity. When that is brushed aside, he accuses his wife of talking like an abolitionist and reminds her that 'pious men' have argued for the justice of slavery. Mrs. Shelby refuses the invitation to argue abstractly. Rather, she points out that there are loving families involved here—human beings she herself has come to love—who care deeply for one another.—Isn't it enough to forbid selling them?—Doesn't moral sensibility give the answer directly?[15]

By suggesting the use of literature to awaken imagination in both students and their teachers, Greene, according to Noddings, provides a possible starting point for critical and moral thinking.

Because passion, for Greene, signifies mood, emotion, and desire, modes of grasping the appearances of things, passion is for her "one of the important ways of understanding possibility".[16] And one way Greene believes students can experience passion is through confrontation with works of art that evoke their emotions. Against this background, educators may also be inspired to search for a critical pedagogy of significance for themselves, consequently rendering conscious, as Greene says, "the process of making meaning, a process that has much to do with the shaping of identity, the development of a sense of agency, and a commitment to a certain mode of praxis".[17]

To better understand the aesthetic illustration of metaphor in Greene's literary practice, I will focus in what follows on several writers who have influenced Greene's work. I will begin with the importance of Nathaniel Hawthorne's short stories. According to Greene, an experience with teaching these texts helped her understand "the ways in which the form of representation feeds the life of meaning. It was not simply a notion of an alternative way of seeing that was important, . . . it was the whole mystery of imaginative literature, the cultural symbol system being tapped, and, in particular, the power of metaphor".[18] The story Greene uses to illustrate her point is that of "The May-Pole of Merry Mount," a tale of two colonies in old New England, the emblem of one being the May-pole, and of the other, the whipping post.[19]

The story opens with the wedding of the Lord and Lady of May on midsummer's eve. Masked figures, a real bear, a mock Indian hunter, a priest with vine leaves in his hair, and others dance around the May-pole. At the climax, Puritans from the nearby colony come to establish their authority over the mirthful sinners, and in so doing to transform the village forever into a land of mournful faces, endless toil, sermon and psalm. The Puritans, never wasting one regretful thought on the vanities of Merry Mount, chop down the May-pole, imprison the dancers, and send the Lord and Lady of May off to heaven.

Hawthorne claimed that he had taken authentic pages from history and that there was indeed a Cavalier colony called Mt. Wollaston.[20] It is therefore possible to teach the story as a version of history, with some elaborations.[21] Yet whether or not the story derives from authentic record, it is presented as a created world, as a world to be brought into existence only as it becomes an object of the reader's experience. This process thus calls for an act of imagination, a deliberate, temporary exclusion of the ordinary and the assumed. Readers who put their own lives into what happens, who shape their experience to accord with the story's symbolic development, who recognize it as

Peace on Earth was all it said
And when I die, when I'm dead + gone, there'll be 1 child born —

to carry on

what Greene calls a "denotative and expressive symbol" that reaches beyond itself, will likely encounter perspectives, openings, and dimensions of experience that reveal themselves in entirely unexpected ways.[22]

For Greene, the implications of Hawthorne's story for a conception of socialization can hardly be ignored. In literal terms, there is first of all the issue of deciding what is being sacrificed when play and dance give way to the demands of responsibility. Since the reader, in order to open the work, must become personally involved with it, his or her consciousness of agency becomes what it ought to become—a matter of existential choosing when a libertine world, primarily occupied with dancing and raising flowers, is made to give way to a life of work.[23] As Greene explains:

> In this kind of fiction, of course, there can be no clear cut either/ors. Looking through the perspectives made available by the work—those of the priest, the dancers with fools caps on their heads, the London minstrels exiled in 'gay despair,' the saddened lady of the May who fancies all the mirth unreal, the zealot Governor Endicott, the 'struggling savage' [whom] the Puritans wanted to shoot down, the unfortunate in the stocks made to dance around the whipping post— readers look upon a world of almost endless variety. There are contradictions, gaps, views from the margin, views from the center; the ordered field thought accurate in its logical or rational representation is now a field of multiplicities. Moreover, the ending holds neither truth nor resolution; like other works of art (and unlike logical arguments) it comes to no firm conclusion. Readers can only attend, perceive particulars, respond emotionally, and interpret what they find against the background of their own lives—made abruptly more visible and more readable than before. It is as if a world opens through the reading of a work of art; readers may see their worlds through it in such a way that horizons broaden and the world seems new, ready to be questioned and explored.[24]

Another author whose work Greene frequently cites is Toni Morrison. Morrison's work, Greene says, "administers amazing shocks that can allow us to develop other modes of recognition against the background of our own lived lives".[25] In the story of Pecola Breedlove in *The Bluest Eye*,[26] for example, Pecola is destroyed by two of the dominant culture's master narratives: the "Dick and Jane" primers and the mythic image of the blue-eyed Shirley Temple. Pecola, a little black girl, unloved by her mother, unsupported by her community, and convinced that she is ugly, wants more than anything to look like Shirley Temple, with her bright blue eyes. If only her eyes were different, she thinks, she herself would be different, and perhaps her parents would no longer do bad things in the presence of such pretty eyes. Eventually, however, Pecola is destroyed and falls into madness. We, as readers, are left with the message that there is only one master story, the implications of which can have destructive results. This novel, Greene suggests, demonstrates the danger of a singular point of view. Instead, Greene writes, "when we see more and hear more, it is not only that we lurch, if only for a moment, out of the familiar and the taken for granted but that new avenues for choosing and for action may open in our experience; we may gain a sudden sense of new beginnings".[27]

As Rebecca Luce-Kapler points out in her essay "The Slow Fuse of Aesthetic Practice," Greene also reads other possibilities into Morrison's novel by focusing on the narrator of the story, Claudia. In the process of telling, Claudia reconfigures her own memories of longing and helplessness in ways that reinterpret her own past and ethnicity.[28] "Whatever meaning she can draw from the connections she makes," Greene writes, "feeds into an ethic that may be meaningful in the future, an ethic that takes her beyond her own guilt at watching Pecola search the garbage".[29] She goes on to say:

> But that is not all. Stories like the one Claudia tells must be able to break through into what we think of as our tradition or our heritage. They will [do so] if we can do what Cornell West has in mind when he speaks about the importance of acknowledging 'the distinctive cultural and political practices of oppressed people' without highlighting their marginality in such a way as to further marginalize them.[30]

Morrison's writings, according to Greene, suggest the never-ending complexity of human beings and human lives and the inevitable incompleteness of all processes of exploration. Her work calls us to experience in new ways the real texture of the human lives that surround and are mediated by our schools, things that cannot be embodied in administrative lists, tables, or reports, or even personal stories. Greene reminds us that some of the tensions people feel may be partially due to suspicion. As she says: "we all often define ourselves against some unknown, some darkness—in many forms, not only of skin color—some 'otherness' that we choose to thrust away, to master rather than to understand".[31]

The novels of Gustave Flaubert, according to Greene, may have a similar effect upon us. Flaubert said he was concerned with the rectification of illusions. He did not simply mean the romantic illusions like those that distorted Emma Bovary's vision of reality; he meant the ideas that fixed the formulas, the conventions that fixed and often falsified dimensions of life and art. To escape fixity, Flaubert thought, life ought to be seen fitfully, in its flow and fragmentation under the corrosions of time. The perverse desires of human beings, the irrational responses, and the irregular and banal rhythms of existence had to be captured in a language properly attuned to the phenomenal world.[32]

Flaubert, like Hawthorne and Morrison, has an ability to move readers to a sense of wide awakeness, and this arousal is for Greene a necessary part of the reader's constructive engagement in a dialectical process of writing and inquiry. For Greene, writing that "breaks forms that have been institutionalized by tradition and privilege suggests a contradictory practice" [33]; this includes, as Greene says, a

> shuttling back and forth between public and private worlds, between subjectivity and objectivity, between experience and narration—the way we actually tend to live our lives. In other words, when we negotiate positions bereft of extremes (i.e., when we are not satisfied to express ourselves in one way *or* the other, but in many ways, all of which acknowledge our identities), we may begin to dislocate positions that privilege tradition and dominant culture. Therefore, pushing back the boundaries of acceptable discourse here can be seen in terms of both the form and content of our language. That is, we challenge the acceptable writing practices/textual authority when the form of our writing is contradictory—when we infuse our language with a personal voice and a presence of persons as Roland Barthes suggests. And we also challenge or question patriarchal tradition (what is taken as given—fixed meanings, fixed social codes, fixed relations of power that beget fixed knowledge and so on) when the content of our writing identifies us with counterhegemonic ideologies or positions that counter dominant perspectives and show the incomplete nature of any particular discourse. [34]

For Greene, multiple meanings and interpretations are central not only to theorizing but to seeing other ways of thinking, acting, and being in the world. She encourages students to read literary texts along such seemingly contradictory lines because she wants to "show the partiality of any single discourse or theory to explain the range of human possibility". [35] As a result, her work empowers people to rediscover their own memories and to articulate them in the presence of others, whose space they can share. But such a project, Greene points out, demands the exercise of imagination enlivened by works of art and by situations of speaking and of making. Perhaps through this we can at last derive reflective communities in the intercises of colleges and schools, freeing people to refuse the silences. As she claims, "we need to teach in such a way as to arouse passion now and then. These are dark and shadowed times and we need to live them, standing before one another open to the world. [36]

By drawing on the above cited works, the point I want to make is that all these writers have the capacity to arouse in their readers a feeling of wide awakeness, an arousal which is a necessity. This dialectical process of writing and inquiry for Greene is both one of contradictory practice and full of contradictions. Like "ethno poetic or involved art," writing for Greene that "breaks forms that have been institutionalized by tradition and privilege suggests a contradictory practice. Writing that infuses the blood and bones of the writer's life with what she or he is writing reconceptualizes the notion of text as involved art, reconceptualizing the purpose of art."[37]

Thus as Greene believes, this contradictory practice of writing and realizing becomes a search for authenticity in a "self whose goal is not power over others but the desire to understand and invoke complicity."[38] Moreover, it is through this same search for authenticity that teachers should approach their teaching—the same practice that helps them to have the courage to tell personal stories in order to help students think through particular theoretical constructs. "Because searching for authenticity or sense of self with others may be the way many of us imagine the possible and analyze the stories of our lives all the time. As it's through a search for authenticity and selfhood that we gain perhaps the deepest understanding of others."[39]

Greene's advocacy is toward a dislocation of boundaries—a blurring of genres—in order to move away from either/or extremes that limit voice and tend to produce totalitarian discourse. By incorporating diverse literary texts into her academic discourse, in essence Greene is questioning the homogenization and standardization of language in the mass media, the schools, and other cultural sites. Implicit in her imaginative literary discourse is the centrality of the arts in school curricula. According to Greene, if we want the arts to help in disclosures and to promote critical awareness, if we want students to experience "the radical modification in the tension of consciousness that enables them to see what they would not otherwise see (as we make available a wide range of art forms), we surely need to keep the questions open and alive."[40]

In conclusion, I have tried in this chapter to elucidate the way in which Greene, through incorporating diverse literary texts into her pedagogical discourse, questions the homogenization and standardization of language in the mass media, the schools, and other cultural sites. Her imaginative literary discourse is predicated on the centrality of the arts in school curricula. Greene embraces the fact that through the awareness of aesthetic images students "can break with the taken for granted, with the ordinary and the mundane".[41] Our role as educators then, should be to encourage our students to become reflective thinkers. As Greene states:

> There must be attending, there must be noticing, at once there must be a reflective turning back to the stream of consciousness—the stream that contains our reflections, our perceptions, our ideas. I am arguing for self reflectiveness and new disclosures, as I am arguing for critical reflection at a moment of crystallized habits. If the uniqueness of the artistic-aesthetic can be reaffirmed, if we can consider futuring as we combat immersion, old either/ors may disappear. We may make possible a pluralism of visions, a multiplicity of realities. We may enable those we teach to rebel.[42]

And indispensable to the development of such a progressive classroom is opening channels of communication that permit students to utilize the linguistic and cultural capital through which they give meaning to their everyday experiences. This means that students must be encouraged to recognize and interrogate the historical, semiotic, and relational dynamics involved in the production of diverse languages. As educators, Greene would like to see teachers make the full range of symbolic systems available to the young for the ordering of their own experience, by encouraging multiple readings of written texts and of the world, readings always unfinished and grounded in possibility. As she says:

> I believe that teachers can release persons for this kind of seeing if we ourselves are able to recover and help our students discover the imaginative mode of awareness that makes the arts available. This is the point of the creative activities we foster in our classrooms and of the creative encounters we try to nurture with works of art. If we do not do our work intentionally, if we do not have a clear sense of what aesthetic perceptions and aesthetics objects signify, we are likely to deprive our students of possibilities. We may leave them buried in cotton wool, and passive under the hammer blows of the fragmented, objective world.[43]

Greene believes that once the students' spontaneity is nurtured and once young people are offered various opportunities to articulate their voices, new possibilities open. At that point, what is offered in terms of subject matter can be grasped more easily, since it is grasped from a lived location, grasped not as a given but from a point of view.[44] And while such manifold student discourses always remain unfinished, they do offer new categories, hope, and commitment to the process of change to educators who believe that schools can in fact be changed and that their individual and collective actions can help deepen and extend democracy and social justice in society at large. The following chapter will discuss how such a democratic reality, one which is not based on the objective, universalized rules defined by the language of the majority, can be achieved.

NOTES

1. Trinh Minh-ha, *When the Moon Waxes Red* (Routledge, 1991), 228229.
2. Maxine Greene, "In Search of a Critical Pedagogy," in *Breaking Free: The Transformative Power of Critical Pedagogy*, eds. Pepi Leistyna, Arlie Woodrum, and Stephen A. Sherblum (Cambridge, Mass.: Harvard Educational Review, 1996), 13.
3. Maxine Greene, "Metaphors and Multiples: Representation, the Arts, and History," *Phi Delta Kappan* (January 1997). 390–391

4. Jean-Paul Sartre, *What is Literature*, (New York: Philosophical Library, 1949), 37.

5. See Maxine Greene, "Literature, Existentialism and Education," in *Existentialism and Phenomenology in Education: Collected Essays*, ed. David Denton (New York: Teachers College Press, 1974).

6. Ibid., 80.

7. Ibid., 76.

8. Maxine Greene, *Landscapes of Learning* (New York: Teachers College Press, 1978), 69.

9. Ibid., 176.

10. Maxine Greene, "Foreword," in *Inquiry and Reflection: Framing Narrative Practice in Education*, ed. Diane Dubose Brunner (Albany: State University of New York Press, 1994), xiv.

11. Greene, "Literature, Existentialism and Education," 80.

12. Ibid., 20.

13. Greene, *Landscapes of Learning*, 39.

14. Nel Noddings, "Ethics and Imagination," in *A Light in Dark Time: Maxine Greene and the Unfinished Conversation*, eds. W. Ayers and Janet L. Miller.

15. Ibid., 169.

16. Greene, "In Search of a Critical Pedagogy," 14.

17. Greene, "Metaphors and Multiples: Representation, the Arts, and History," pp. 390–391

18. Ibid.

19. Nathaniel Hawthorne, "The May-Pole of Merry Mount," in *Selected Tales and Sketches* (New York: Penguin Books, 1987). 138–149

20. See Greene, "Metaphors and Multiples: Representation, the Arts, and History."

21. Ibid.

22. Ibid.

23. Ibid.

24. Ibid., 6.

25. Greene, *Releasing the Imagination: Essays on Education, Arts, and Social Change*, (San Francisco: Jossey-Base Publishers, 1995) 118.

26. Toni Morrison, *The Bluest Eye* (New York: Bantam Books, 1970).

27. ibid., 123.

28. See Rebecca Luce-Kapler, "The Slow Fuse of Aesthetic Practice," in *The Passionate Mind of Maxine Greene: I am . . . not Yet*, ed. William F. Pinar.

29. Greene, *Releasing the Imagination*, 125.

30. Ibid., 165.

31. Greene, *Releasing the Imagination*, 162

32. See Greene, *Landscapes of Learning*.

33. Greene, "Foreword," in *Inquiry and Reflection*, xv.

34. Ibid., xvi

35. Ibid.

36. Greene, "In Search of a Critical Pedagogy," 29.

37. Greene, "Foreword," in *Inquiry and Reflection*, xv.

38. Ibid., xviii.

39. Ibid., xvi.

40. Greene, *Landscapes of Learning*, 175.

41. Greene, *Landscapes of Learning.*, 181.

42. Ibid., 182.

43. Ibid., 186.

44. See Maxine Greene, "The Lived World," in, ed. Lynda Stone (New York: Routledge Press, 1994).

Chapter Four

The Limits of Universality: Delimiting the Standardized Curriculum

From the previous chapters, we can conclude that, for Greene, any adequate program of teacher education or teacher research must begin with hard questions arising out of a race, class, and gender-conscious, self-critical, awareness and extending to wider political contexts that include issues of knowledge, power, voice, and position. This dialectical discourse manifests itself in every situation, especially in the matter of those students who are otherwise marginalized by an overarching standard curriculum. This concept of different ways of knowing is emphasized throughout Greene's philosophy and is pivotal in her understanding of education. As she states in *Landscapes of Learning*:

> I believe that there must be an affirmation of a pluralistic concern as this uncovering proceeds. Such an affirmation demands a new recognition of community. There must be a perception of the ways in which persons locate themselves in the world in the light of their own particular biographical situations, the experience they build over time. Every individual interprets the realities he or she confronts through perspectives made up of particular ranges of interests, occupations, commitments and desires. Each one belongs to a number of social groups and plays a variety of social roles. Their individual involvements effects the 'stock of knowledge at hand." Particular persons make use of it in order to interpret from particular vantage points; as they do so, a common meaning structure is built up among them, they share a common world.[1]

Greene's point is that students come from diverse angles and vantage points. And the curriculum should reflect this common meaning structure from all these perspectives. In this chapter, I will show how curriculum making and institutions of higher learning, by assuming the neutral stance of an universal curriculum discriminate against those students whose voices are not

Not ours to own
— but our future

included it. Because the process of attempting to define the curriculum within a universal "standardized" system inevitably leaves out, downplays, or attempts to suppress real difference among particular entities, the language of such a curriculum in this context privileges "objectivity and rights over their binary opposites, subjectivity and responsibility".[2] This differentiation is implied through a silencing of difference in a supposedly neutral language of "impartiality."

The so-called neutral stances that produce academic standards exist only through an abstraction from the specifics of situation, feeling, affiliation, and point of view. These specifics still obtain, however, in the actual context of action. Thus, the so-called standardization gives rise to a dichotomy between the universal and the particular, between private and public, and between reason and passion. The ideal serves only the political function of disguising the ways in which the perspectives of dominant groups claim universality, thus rationalizing monolithic decision-making structures.[3]

In line with Greene, I will argue that it is necessary to replace language that denies body and feeling, as does the still dominant curriculum discourse of standardization, with a new and distinctive expressiveness. This different imaginary position, moreover, should be used to describe curriculum discourse in terms of personal experiences.

Unless the language of curriculum discourse is reformulated to include individual voices, education and the educational system will always fail to protect individual rights. As Greene herself states, "The responsibility of a teacher is to work for 'a more authentic speaking' to combat mystification"[4] and standardization in curriculum theory. Consequently, "the problem of language used by teachers is as crucial as the problem of categories devised for organizing what is known".[5] The responsibility of a teacher is to make sure that students are able to speak in their own voices, thereby simultaneously constructing and expressing their identities through various idioms and styles.

As part of my discussion, I will also explore the work of curriculum theorists such as Madeline Grumet, William Pinar, and Max van Manen, whose work, although different in their apparent emphasis, reflects a similar underlying concern that is pivotal in Greene's pedagogy, namely, that of interpreting curriculum within a pluralistic context. The purpose of undertaking an examination of the theories of these writers is to explore how their curriculum pedagogies have successfully incorporated a democratic participatory theory of education such as Greene advocates, one that includes a notion of curriculum that caters to the various entities and vantage points involved.

According to Edward Said:

When our students are taught such things as the humanities they are almost always taught that these classic texts embody, express, represent what is best in our, that is, the only tradition. Moreover, they are taught that such fields as the humanities and such sub fields such as literature exist in a relatively neutral political element, that they are to be appreciated and venerated and that they define the limits of what is acceptable, appropriate and legitimate as far as how curriculum is defined.[6]

The fact that other traditions, other voices, are not included is seldom if ever questioned within this tradition. As a result, this dominant mode of categorization of reality is internalized by students, even those whose voices and histories have been absent from the canon. Once internalized, notions like subordination, natural inferiority, and unequally distributed rights are taken for granted. These constructs come to be seen as objective characteristics of an objective, existent world. However, a definition of reality that operates by reducing difference to a set of common characteristics denies the importance of the contextuality of particular relationships.

This process, moreover, generates dichotomies rather than unity, because the effort to bring particulars under a universal category gives rise to a distinction between what is considered primary and what is considered secondary within the curriculum discourse. But since each particular entity or situation has both similarities and differences with other particular entities or situations, and they are neither fully the same nor completely other; the urge to bring them together under a single category or principle entails excluding some of them altogether. Since the totalizing movement always leaves a remainder, the attempt to reduce particulars to a unity must always fail. The logic of sameness, rather than admit defeat in the face of difference, endeavors to force difference into dichotomous hierarchical oppositions: essence/ accident, good/bad, normal/deviant.[7]

The first term in each of these dichotomies is validated at the expense of the second because it is claimed to designate the unified and the self-identical. In every case, the unity supposedly named under of the "positive" term is achieved only at the expense of expelling and failing to account for a chaotic realm of the accidental. Difference, however, subverts the claim that "this is all there is;" the trace of otherness remains. The bearers of the marginalized characteristics are nonetheless subordinated as impure examples of something that they are not, excluded as other. As Iris Young says, the very construction of the categories habitually designated by such oppositions depends upon valuing what lies inside over what lies outside[8] curriculum discourse. One of the results is that the meta-narrative in education that separates the universal from the particular, the public from the private, generates such central concepts as "civility" and citizenship, concepts that repress the self-expression of such marginalized groups as women and minorities.

In sharp contrast to Sartre, Greene by situating herself within a particularized context, namely that of a woman, resituates philosophy on gendered terrain, what Mary-Ellen Jacobs has called a "honeycomb of hills and valleys."[9] A context that reflects how her emerging understanding of herself as a philosopher and as a woman is marked by difference. As Greene herself states:

> I want to discuss the lived world and the perceptual realities of women because I am so sharply aware of the degrees to which they are obscured by sex and gender roles. I am convinced that the imposition of these roles makes women falsify their sense of self. Patriarchal culture—a culture that defines women as other—denies women their perceptions of the live world and instead confines them into their socially prescribed roles daughter wife mother. Roles themselves are social constructs that compel us, regardless of gender, to adapt ourselves to the reality of others. In doing so, we are likely to lose touch with our projects, to become invisible . . . to think of ourselves as others define us, not as we create ourselves.[10]

Historical reality for women, however, ensures that the particularities of everyday life are inescapable.[11] They lack the option merely to claim their freedom and their rights and avoid the realms of obligation and concern. To do so can lead them to alienate themselves from the very ground of their being.[12]

Women claim their freedom only by engaging in an existential struggle. But this struggle cannot occur in a vacuum. Freedom cannot be conceived independent of the matrix of social, economic, cultural, and psychological conditions. It is within this matrix that the individual takes shape or is created, through choice of action in the changing situations of life. The degree and quality of any freedom that is achieved emerge as reflections of the perspectives that are available and of the choices that are made within this intersubjective labyrinth.

For Simone de Beauvoir, the dethroning of "the myth of femininity" is a necessary step in the dismantling of patriarchy.[13] According to de Beauvoir, it is evident that women, once freed from complicity in the perpetuation of their own oppression and from economic subordination, will find their opportunity to achieve full membership in the human race. De Beauvoir apparently assumes that women are no different from men, and that it is only men's false projection of women that obscures this fact. But to seek to escape myth, especially myths of the feminine, is to once again re-instate the neutral concept of person. As de Beauvoir believes, the myth can be dethroned if we can finally raise the veil and see that women are fully human — by this she implies that we have to see women like men. But if we are to follow de Beauvoir's line of reasoning, overcoming the gender mechanism only reinstates it. The gender hierarchy itself perpetuates the myth, and we can neither simply erase the myth nor dethrone it. Our only option is to work within the myth by investigating what is particular to women's moral development, ethics, and modes of knowing.

Consequently, women have to dialectically engage with the determining forces around them and to realize that freedom can only be achieved in an ongoing transaction, one that is visible and legible to those involved. The road to freedom for Greene can only be opened when women become aware of alternative possibilities for themselves.

Greene goes on to criticize the public institution system in its so-called protection of rights of women. She challenges the paradigm of moral reasoning as defined by the discourse of Aristotelian justice and by the notion of "impartial rights" that speak from a supposedly neutral perspective. Women's experience, according to Greene, cannot be defined in terms of abstract rights:

> We have to acknowledge as well that the language and the arguments devised by the campaigners for women's suffrage tended to be the language and arguments of liberal individualism. They were developed in the tradition of male autonomy and self determination central to the public sphere males inhabited in contradistinction from the private sphere. Now the women proponents of equal rights would seek independence from men in a realm apart from male domination or the 'aristocracy of sex' but they would call for its constitution in universalistic, not particularists terms . . . .[B]ecause the public space was the arena where rational capacities could be realized, and there the good could be given objective status, and because men were the actors in that space, it followed that those excluded were considered less than human in the generic sense.[14]

Elsewhere she states that:

> We [must] understand that a mere removal of constraint or a mere relaxation of controls will not ensure the emergence of free and creative human beings. We understand that the freedom we cherish is not an endowment, that it must be achieved through dialectical engagements with the social and economic obstacles we find standing in our way, those we have to learn to name. We understand that a plurality of voices must be attended to, a plurality of life stories must be heeded if a meaningful power is to spring up through a new 'binding and promising, combining and covenanting.'[15]

A free act, according to Greene, unlike an abstraction from a master script, is a particularized one. It is undertaken from the standpoint of a particular, situated person trying to bring into existence something contingent on his or her hopes, expectations, and capacities. The world in which a person creates and works through a future project cannot but be a social world; and the nature of the project cannot but be affected by shared meanings and interpretations of existing social realities.

Anita Plath Helle, in her essay "Reading Women's Autobiographies: A Map of Reconstructed Knowing," says that collective thought and action require a continued critique of the exclusive reliance on separate knowing that has presented epistemic barriers to women.[16] She further states that:

> Theoretical discourse has typically been defined as language held by those in power, and it has often structured our reality by pointing to fixed and impartial frames of reference. . . . Once such references become part of a cultural code, they operate unconsciously to constrain rather than to liberate the construction of alternative standpoints (Eagleton, 1983). . . . To mix languages, to blend differences is thus to struggle to produce change from within *and* outside procedures that constrain us.[17]

Through the process of discourse we can discover the terms or formal problems through which women are constituted. An interpretation of women through discourse will thus decategorize the gender hierarchy, and revealing an indeterminacy in which we can never know once and for all who or what woman is, imposed categories in which we confront her being, after all, always open to revisions and reinterpretations.

Within this framework, dialogue becomes an ongoing process, and in each moment of discourse old sedimentations of language are eroded away at the same time as new perceptions are created. Through engagement in this process, men and women alike are creating their own language out of the other's indeterminacy and difference. At the same time, by engaging in dialogue with the other, they acknowledge the other as other than themselves. True identity for the first time emerges in difference, and at last the other is not an extension of the self. Greene reinforces this discourse framework in her discussion of multiple dialogues:

> If spaces of dialogue can extend far enough and connect to other spaces, if diverse human voices can become more and more audible, if more and more publics can be formed and become articulate, the mystifying languages will become in some manner transparent. We will hear articulations of new visions as possibilities open, as people begin to recognize the incompleteness of things.[18]

Consequently, designating autobiographical and context-specific discourse as a ground for social transformation of the public sphere is integral to a dialectical politics of freedom and possibility, because it is in a constructed discourse of experience and language that we find, as Greene believes, both our subordination and our strength. We must at all times, Greene states:

> remember that the reality in question is a constructed one. Only as people come to understand that they need not accede to the world as demarcated and named by others, will they acknowledge that things can be different. Acknowledging that, they will be free to point to insufficiencies of the kind the school reformers so easily obscured. Acknowledging that, they may also be free to engage in the modes of dialogue needed for reconstituting what exists. Here is where the "art of full and moving communication comes to play". The communication must be of the kind that enables each participant to find his or her own singular and authentic voice in the progress of identifying values common to all, ideals that are shared. Existing with each other, committed to realizing a good shared by all, men and women, girls and boys, may be empowered to constitute democracy.[19]

Learning to conceptualize educational arguments in a dialogical framework of this kind would give birth to a significant methodological and substantive mechanism for subjecting stagnant universal interpretations of curriculum to the corrective effects of deviation. Dialogue that incorporates both legal arguments and a pluralistic notion of social interrelationships into a critique of a standardized curriculum would be a boon to the undoing of its repressive component. If academic reason is dialogical, emerging from discussion among differently situated subjects, subjects who all require the recognition and acknowledgment of others, then there is no need for a universal point of view to awaken people from their egoism.

In what follows, I will examine whether existing institutions and the culture of standardized curriculum can be changed via an existentialist discourse as defined by curriculum theorists like William Pinar, Madeline Grumet, and Max van Manen.

Pinar points out that critical theory and phenomenology are movements in philosophy, not in curriculum theory or practice, and claims that while understanding of such work is necessary, a retreat to the explication of philosophical texts represents an evasion of our professional responsibility as educators.[20] Van Manen supports Pinar's claim when he emphasizes that a strong educational theory does not depend upon philosophical analysis of curriculum; instead a strong theory is one that is committed to promoting the pedagogic good. By pedagogic good he refers to "the end . . . from which all hope, love and inspiration for our children draws its meaning".[21]

Influenced by the Utrecht school, van Manen asserts that pedagogy encompasses the entire realm of lifeworld issues that surface in teacher-student and adult-child relationships. The Utrecht theorists are known for their method of structural exposition called "situation analysis." This investigative procedure works through a careful study of concrete examples supplied by experience or imagination, and is believed by followers to allow one to gain insight into the significant structures and relationships of pedagogical experience.[22]

The issues arising from these relationships can range from questions of curriculum and learning methodology to the pedagogical responsibilities of the parent vis-à-vis the child. Pedagogy, in this sense, is then a particular normative stance one takes in the world toward children.[23] Van Manen writes:

> As new parents, before we have a chance to sit back and reflect on whether we can accept this child, the child has already made us act. And luckily for humankind, this spontaneous needfulness to do the right thing is usually the right thing. As we reach to hold the child . . ., we have already acted pedagogically. This is our practical 'knowledge' of pedagogy. . . . In other words, as soon as we gain a lived sense of the pedagogic quality of parenting and teaching, we start to question and doubt ourselves. Pedagogy is this questioning, this doubting. We wonder: Did I do the right thing? Why do some people teach or bring their children up in such a different manner? [24]

In his recent writings, van Manen, in describing the pedagogical interactions between parent and child and between teacher and child, focuses on the lived experiences of individual students. Particularly important in this context, naturally, are those everyday experiences that relate to pedagogical concerns. As van Manen writes:

> As we research the possible meaning structure of our lived experiences, we come to a fuller grasp of what it means to be in the world as a man, a woman, a child, taking into account the sociocultural and the historical traditions which have given meaning to our ways of being in the world.[25]

Consequently, pedagogical theorizing is for van Manen a bringing into reflective awareness of everyday lived experience in a textual process. As he says:

> Pedagogy requires a phenomenological sensitivity to lived experience (children's realities and life worlds). Pedagogy requires a hermeneutic ability to make interpretive sense of the phenomena of the life world in order to see the pedagogic significance of situations and relations of living with children. Any pedagogy requires a way with language in order to allow the research process of textual reflection to contribute to one's pedagogic thoughtfulness and tact.[26]

Theoretical knowledge and diagnostic information, however, do not guarantee appropriate pedagogical practices. Rather, according to van Manen, pedagogy manifests its true nature in the practical moment of concrete situations. Knowledge necessary for pedagogical action must therefore be situation-specific and centered upon the individual child concerned. Pedagogy, in other words, is context-sensitive.[27]

For van Manen, pedagogy is always concerned with the question of what one ought to know, what one ought to be able to do, and what kind of person one ought to be in order to provide focus for and deal appropriately with given children in given pedagogical situations. It is usually quite impossible, however, to deal with concrete pedagogical relations unless one has some understanding of their context. Teachers who are pedagogically sensitive to the children they work with also tend to be sensitive to the particular backgrounds, life histories, qualities, and circumstances of the children in question.[28] As a result, pedagogical reflection on action can be said to render the actions themselves more thoughtful and sensitive.[29] This capacity for mindful action van Manen refers to as pedagogical tact.[30]

Tact for van Manen is the practical language of the body—it is the language of acting in the context of the pedagogical moment. Tactful action is direct involvement in situations in which the educator must respond immediately and as a whole person to unexpected and unpredictable situations. Tact, as experienced in pure active living with children, is the conscious awareness of our subjective self as we act. In other words, while we are acting as teachers or as parents with children, we do not objectify or establish distance from our actions. As van Manen says:

> Tact as a form of human interaction means that we are immediately active in a situation: emotionally, responsively, mindfully. Even when as tactful pedagogues we are engaged sensitively, reflecting with a child—searching for the right thing to say or do, we nevertheless are only dimly aware of our actions, . . . And, therefore, philosophically speaking, our thinking, feeling, acting is relatively attenuated, drawn in, limited, or restrained by the possibilities.[31]

No quality is more essential for the practice of pedagogical understanding than a capacity for trustful sympathy. Pedagogical understanding commonly occurs as an immediate comprehension of what is going on with a child. Simply to diagnose or evaluate a child's state of education, however, is not sufficient. Educational understanding becomes pedagogical understanding only when it focuses on working out what it means for this particular child to be and to become an educated person in the context of his or her evolving life. Thus, educational/pedagogical understanding has to surpass the mere diagnostic or evaluative assessment of what a given child possesses or still needs.

It must also be able to appraise the strengths and weaknesses not only in the child's educational achievements, but in his or her social and emotional development as well.

Similarly to van Manen, Pinar and Grumet have devised a method by means of which the educational researcher can scrutinize his or her own limit situations, his or her own role in fixed social and psychological structures, and his or her passive acquiescence in the chilling of intellectual development that typifies American schooling.[32] Essential to the formulation worked out by these authors is an acknowledgment of the deception inherent in the duality of "self" and "world." Following the existentialist themes of Greene and van Manen, human beings, for Pinar and Grumet, are irrevocably "beings in the world." The world is both cause and consequence of the conditioned and of the chosen in human life. [33]

According to Madeline Grumet, in order for a curriculum to supply the ethical and epistemological, let alone the social situations that allow students to articulate their own points of view, it must provide grounds upon which they can act, not simply acquiesce.[34] Curriculum, as Grumet says:

> is a moving form. That is why we have trouble capturing it, fixing it in language, lodging it in our matrix. Whether we talk about it as history, as syllabi, as classroom discourse, as intended learning outcome, or as experience, we are trying to grasp a moving form, to catch it at the moment that it slides from the figure, the object and goal of action, and collapses into the ground for action. Through its movement curriculum intertwines the actual and the ideal. . . . Curriculum considered apart from its appropriation and transformation by students, curriculum defined as design, a structure of knowledge, an intended learning outcome, or a learning environment is merely a static form.[35]

By concentrating on the students' biographies and life worlds, Grumet and Pinar examine the ways in which these disciplines provide metaphors for daily experience. In their book, *Toward a Poor Curriculum*,[36] a collection of essays in which Pinar and Grumet examine and promote the use of autobiographical accounts of educational experiences as resources for educational research and theory, the authors challenge the dominance of quantitative methods of inquiry and of education. As an alternative, they present philosophy and literature as traditions in the humanities that use narrative to order and express experience. Pinar and Grumet's emphasis, in contrast to the anonymity and standardization of the quantitative research model, is on the biography of the individual writer, on the appropriateness of everyday experience as a context for knowledge, and on the ability of the narrative form to transmit the essence of educational experience. From this perspective, education can be clearly understood as a metaphor for individual discourse and individual identity.[37]

Pedagogy of this kind is grounded in relations and in dialogue. When educators and researchers employ autobiographical methods of inquiry, they themselves can become both the subject and the object of research. The reflexive process that Pinar suggests would also positively influence the developmental capacity to reach back through our experience to the preconceptual encounters upon which our judgments are based. According to Pinar, when we misunderstand ourselves, we misunderstand the world. Through this focus on autobiography, he describes a research method that would encompass a phenomenological description of subject and object, requiring knowledge of self as knower of the world.[38]

Autobiographical methods, moreover, are rooted in context. Through them we represent ourselves, as in existential phenomenology, in situation. As Pinar states:

> We are not mere smudges on the mirror. Our life stories are not liabilities to be exorcised but are the very precondition for knowing. It is our individual and collective stories in which the present projects are situated, and it is awareness of these stories which is the lamp illuminating the dark spots, the rough edges.[39]

The approach of scaling the inquiry down to the experiential field of the individual Pinar calls *currere*, which he explains is the Latin root of the word *curriculum*. Its study involves investigation of the nature of the individual experience of the public.[40] As he says, "It is by the experience and ideas through which I am marginalized, and or through which I choose to dwell in the margins, that I experience the public as an individual. And it is from that experience that I gain multiple perspectives around notions of self, other, and society as both separate and connected". Pinar adds:

> *Currere* refers to my existential experience of external structures. The method of currere is a strategy devised to disclose this experience, so that we may see it more clearly. With such seeing can come deepened understanding of the running, and with this, can come deepened agency. We must make use of autobiographical reflection to penetrate our public masks, which keep us disconnected from our experience.[41]

Currere responds to the traditional empirical curriculum paradigm with a call for a return to the experience of the individual.[42] Currere, as an autobiographical process, consists in reflection and analysis such that one recalls and examines one's educational experience. This is something the individual does with the curriculum, now actively reconstructing his or her journey through its social, intellectual, and physical structures.[43]

In looking at currere as a developmental process that addresses the dichotomy of the individual and humanity at large, Grumet and Pinar see currere as an adjunct to conventional teaching. The authors describe a research method in which currere is not a reflective retreat from the world but a process that perceives and interacts with the world without appropriating it. Thus, the method constitutes both an encounter with objectivity and a microcosm, in which, unlike the constant flux we see around us, the permanence of the written word is primary, making the examined world accessible to other subjectivities and to future encounters:[44]

> The first step of currere is the regressive association of the past. We work to excavate the present by working on the past, work to get underneath my everyday interpretation of what I experience, and enter experience more deeply. The next step, the progressive, asks me to ponder meditatively the future, in order to uncover my aspiration, in order to ascertain where I am moving. Third I analyze what I uncover in the first two sections, an analysis devoted to intuitive comprehension as well as cognitive codifications. I work to get a handle on what I've been and what I imagine myself to be, so that I can wield this information rather than it wielding me.[45]

Educational experience, if interpreted within such an existentialist context, is a process that projects the self into the world without dismembering that self, a process of synthesis and totalization in which all the participants in the dialectic simultaneously maintain their identities and surpass themselves. It is above all a process of talking of education as a dialogue between person and world, rather than breaking down this complex interaction into separate parts, subjecting each to a distinct, isolated analysis.

In conclusion, this chapter has stressed that our exploration of the notion of pedagogy thus far may suggest that pedagogical fitness assumes a sense of vocation, love, and caring for children, "a deep sense of responsibility and of active hope in the face of prevailing crises, a reflective maturity, a pedagogical understanding based on a capacity to listen to and 'see' children, and a generally trustful, sympathetic attitude toward young people".[46] Teaching within this context was discussed as both a public and a private activity, calling on both narrative and analytical ways of knowing. This asks us to address both moral and aesthetic values, as well as the practical aspects of everyday experience.

The two major realities that confront the curricular worker are the activities within a classroom—or activities designated in other ways as educational—and the existential situation of choice as interpreted by various differing communities. The next chapter attempts to answer the underlying question "What would an emancipatory discipline of curriculum, one which is based on an existentialist concept of freedom, look like within a classroom setting?" By offering concrete suggestions to teachers and educators as to how to implement an existentialist curriculum within a classroom setting, the concluding chapter contextualizes Greene's existential theory within a curriculum of democratic action and within the specificity of a community.

NOTES

1. Maxine Greene, *Landscapes of Learning* (New York: Teachers College Press), 69–70.

2. D. Cole, "Strategies of Difference: Litigating for Women's Rights in a Man's World," *Law and Inequality: Journal of Theory and Practice* 2 (February 1984): 45.

3. See Iris Marion Young, *Justice and the Politics of Difference* (New Jersey: Princeton University Press 1990).

4. Greene, *Landscapes of Learning*, 54.

5. Ibid., 104.

6. Edward W. Said, *The World, the Text, the Critic* (Cambridge, MA: Harvard University Press 1983), 21.

7. Young, *Justice and the Politics of Difference* 99.

8. Ibid., 102.

9. Mary-Ellen Jacobs, "Living Dangerously: Towards a Poetics of Women's Lived Experience," in *A Light in Dark Times*, 180.

10. Maxine Greene, "How I Came to Phenomenology," *Phenomenology and Pedagogy* 1 (1983), 3.

11. Maxine Greene, *Dialectic of Freedom* (New York: Teachers College Press, 1988), 71.

12. Ibid., 71.

13. See Simone de Beauvoir, *The Second Sex* translated and edited by H. M. Parshley (New York: Alfred A. Knopf, 1953).

14. Greene, *The Dialectic of Freedom*, 69.

15. Greene, "In Search of a Critical Pedagogy," in *Breaking Free: The Transformative Power of Critical Pedagogy*, eds. Pepi Leistyna, Arlie Woodrum, and Stephen A. Sherblum (Cambridge, Mass.: Harvard Educational Review, 1996), 29.

16. Anita Plath Helle, "Reading Women's Autobiographies: A Map of Reconstructed Knowing," in Nel Noddigs and Carol Witherall (eds.) *Stories Lives Tell: Narrative and Dialogue in Education* (New York: Teachers College Press, 1991), 63.

17. Ibid. See also Terry Eagleton, *Literary Theory: An Introduction* (Minneapolis: University of Minnesota Press, 1983).

18. Maxine Greene, "Public Spaces in Local Places," *Phenomenology and Pedagogy* 10 (1992): 249.

19. Greene, *Landscapes of Learning*, 123.

20. William Pinar, "Notes on the Curriculum Field" (1978), in his *Autobiography, Politics and Sexuality: Essays in Curriculum Theory 1972–1992* (New York: Peter Lang Press, 1994), 89.

21. Max van Manen, "Edifying Theory; Serving the Good," *Theory into Practice* (1982) 21/1, 47.

22. See Max van Manen, "The Utrecht School; An Experiment in Educational theorizing," *Interchange* (1979) 10/1, 48–66. See also Robert K. Brown, "Max Manen and Pedagogical Human Science Research," in *Understanding Curriculum as Phenomenological and Deconstructed Text*, eds. William. F. Pinar and William M. Reynolds (New York: Teachers College Press, 1992), 44–63.

23. Brown, "Max Manen and Pedagogical Human Science Research" 46.

24. Max van Manen, "The Relation between Research and Pedagogy," in *Contemporary Curriculum Discourses*, edited by William F. Pinar. (Scottsdale, Ariz.: Gorsuch Scarisbrick, 1988). 447.

25. Max van Manen, "Practical Phenomenological Writing," *Phenomenology and Pedagogy* 2/1, 3639. Quoted in Brown, 51

26. Max van Manen, *Researching Lived Experience: Human Science from an Action Sensitive Pedagogy* (London, Ontario: Althouse Press, 1988). Quoted in Brown, 52.

27. Max van Manen, *The Tact of Teaching: The Meaning of pedagogical Thoughtfulness* (Albany: State University of New York Press, 1991), 47.

28. Ibid., 48.

29. Ibid., 117.

30. Ibid., 122.

31. Ibid.

32. See Madeline R. Grumet, *Bitter Milk: Women and Education* (Amherst: The University of Massachusetts Press, 1988).

33. See Pinar, "Notes on the Curriculum Field," in *Autobiography, Politics and Sexuality* (1983), 90.

34. Grumet, *Bitter Milk*, 172.

35. Ibid., 173.

36. William F. Pinar and Madeline R. Grumet, *Toward a Poor Curriculum* (Dubuque, Iowa: Kendall Hunt Publishing Company, 1976).

37. Madeline R. Grumet, "Existential and Phenomenological Foundations of Autobiographical Methods," in *Understanding Curriculum as a Racial Text: Representations of Identity and Difference in Education*, eds. Louis A. Castenell, Jr. and William F. Pinar, 28.

38. Ibid., 36.

39. Pinar and Grumet, *Towards a Poor Curriculum*, 148.

40. William Pinar and Louis A. Castenell, *Understanding Curriculum as Racial Text: Representations of Identity and Difference* (Albany: State University of New York Press, 1993), 59.

41. Pinar and Grumet, *Towards a Poor Curriculum*, vii.

42. Ibid., 45.

43. Ibid., 111.

44. Ibid., 41.

45. Ibid., ix.

46. van Manen, *The Tact of Teaching*, 123.

Chapter Five

Conclusion: Implications for Educators: Creating Curriculums of Action in the Classroom

In examining the work of Pinar, Grumet and van Manen, the previous chapter suggested that even though these curriculum theorists attempt to account for the creative, aesthetic possibilities of life they do not, like Greene, with her inquiry into the dialectic of freedom, establish a synthesized "democratic" framework for classroom interaction.[1] An important element of curriculum inquiry for Greene is to "affirm that actual practitioners in their diverse communities ought to pose their own questions about what democratic education and democratic citizenship mean and ought to mean in the postmodern time."[2]

According to Greene, discussions of curriculum standards, frameworks, and desired results still have not focused seriously on the matter of our purposes as a society. Nor have they examined what it means to educate live persons, or how to empower the young to go beyond making a living and contributing to the economy to participating in the remaking of their own world.[3]

Through an examination of Greene's educational pedagogy, I have tried to develop an existentialist view of a democratic education of freedom, one that will take into account our political and social realities as well as the existentialist conception of the human condition itself. Through an analysis of Greene's notion of freedom in the various contexts in which it is manifest, I have attempted in this book to explicate her understanding of a democratically liberated consciousness.[4]

From the very beginning of *The Dialectic of Freedom*, Greene remains continuously aware both of the constraints on and positive opportunities for democratic liberation and of the intimate relationship between personal and social freedom.[5] She is aware of the dangers that an over emphasis on plurality can have in creating a democratic culture as she says that: "It is important to hold this in mind as we try to work through a conception of pluralism to an affirmation of the struggle to attain the life of a 'free and enriching commun-ion' John Dewey identified with democracy".[6]

Within such a context Greene urges educators to ask how we can while ed-ucating for freedom, "create and maintain a common world?."[7] In attempting to answer the question she is not suggesting that curricula should be tailored to the measures of specific cultural groups of young people. She is suggest-ing instead a need for, "openness as well as inclusion."[8] Greene believes that individuals living in a democratic society should avoid adhering to cultural stereotypes, including those linked to multiculturalism. In a related quote she states: "While realizing that cultural background plays a part in shaping iden-tity, this culture should never become an absolute, closing the person against the 'new culture surrounding him or her.'"[9]

Concern for pluralism, from Greene's perspective, must be balanced with a commitment to create a unity and cohesion among all who live in our soci-ety. According to her the creative challenge is not to preserve some artificial cultural norm in the face of our increasing diversity, but to establish some means of collective identity that does not undermine our commitment to plu-ralism. Rather than identity a common cultural canon to hold us together, Greene suggests we consider the value of pluralism itself. That is, a recogni-tion by all of the unique strength we have as a nation due to our diversity.[10] The ideal community she states:

> is a community attentive to difference, open to ideals of plurality. Something life affirming in diversity must be discovered and rediscovered, of what is held in common becomes always more multifaceted-open and inclusive, drawn to un-tapped possibility, nor can we absolutely justify one kind of community over an-other. Many of us, however, for all the tensions and disagreements around us, would reaffirm the value of principles like justice and equality and freedom and commitment to human rights since, without these, we cannot even argue for the decency of welcoming.[11]

Community similar to freedom has to be achieved by persons offered the space in which to discover what they recognize together and appreciate in common; they have to find ways to make intersubjective sense. In this sense, existential freedom is both a goal of democratic living and means to creating this life. From Greene's perspective, a fully democratic culture is one that supports, encourages, and celebrates our struggle to be existentially free, that is, to be fully awake. And it is within this context of democratic freedom that education is situated. She believes that if educators are seriously interested in educating for freedom they need to find a way of developing a praxis of ed-ucational consequence, one that opens the spaces necessary for the remaking of a democratic community.[12]

Consequently for Greene, curriculum involves a process of enabling the young to make sense of their personal lived worlds and to build their own interpreted realities within a social order. The social order is crucial here, in that Greene recognizes that self knowledge cannot be cultivated in isolation from others: "the self can never be actualized through solely private experiences, no matter how extraordinary these experiences might be."[13] As she says: "To open up our experience (and, yes, our curriculum) to existential possibilities of multiple kinds is to extend and deepen what each of us thinks of when he or she speaks of a community."[14]

Greene believes that one way teachers can achieve this pluralistic sense of community is if they bring themselves into their schools and use their own lives, their knowledge, and their explorations as elements within the curriculum. She in turn puts this sense of personal connectedness into practice by situating herself as an educator when she says:

> The quest involves me as a woman, as teacher, as mother, as citizen, as New Yorker, as art-lover, as activist, as philosopher, as white middle-class American. Neither myself or my narrative can have, therefore, a single strand. I stand at the crossing point of too many social and cultural forces; and in any case, I am forever on the way.[15]

Consequently Greene advocates the encouragement of a dialogical "self-reflection" in teacher education curricula: "I am proposing . . . that teacher educators and their students be stimulated to think about their own thinking and to reflect upon their own reflecting".[16] As Greene says:

> I am convinced that through reflective and impassioned teaching we can do far more to excite and stimulate many sorts of young persons to reach beyond themselves, to create meanings, to look through wider and more informed perspectives at the actualities of their lived lives. It seems eminently clear to me that a return to a single standard of achievement and a one-dimensional definition of the common will not only result in severe injustices to the children of the poor and the dislocated, the children at risk, but will also thin out our cultural life and make it increasingly difficult to bring into existence and keep alive an authentically common world. Granted, multiple perspective, make it all the more difficult to define coherent purposes in what many believe to be a dangerously fragmented culture, devoid of significant guidelines and generally accepted norms. Multiplicity makes it difficult as well to think about how we can love our children in Arendt's terms and remain true to what we have come to know as practitioners.[17]

Greene goes on to say that many of the alienated students are forced into the position of distrusting their own voices, their own ways of making sense. At the same time, they are provided with no alternatives to allow them to otherwise tell their stories, formulate their narratives, or contextualize new learning within the sphere of what they already know.

Within this context the existentialist educator comes face to face with his or her freedom, as well as with the dispossessed freedoms of his or her students; If the teacher orchestrates experiences that pose problems that are substantively and qualitatively different from those posed in the past, the students, if they in turn have developed the necessary powers and can see the significance of these new problems, will find that they perceive more and more alternative solutions. Thus, they will evaluate the world of choice and of action more creatively and effectively. In other words, they will grow.[18]

As discussed in the previous chapters, Greene, inspired by the arts and humanities, challenges educators to think of their work in imaginative, poetic, and narrative idioms. Regarding the importance of infusing arts in the curriculum, she states: "to speak of the arts in relation to curriculum inquiry is, for me, to summon up visions of new perspectives and untapped possibilities. Curriculum has to do with the life of meaning, with ambiguities, and with relationships. And, yes it has to do with transformations and with fluidity".[19]

With reference to the search for meaning, which is a central motif of inquiry both in the arts and in curriculum theory, Greene believes that educators have a special role to play. According to Greene, educators must "feel the importance of releasing students to be personally present to what they see and hear and read . . . [to] develop a sense of agency and participation and [to] do so in collaboration with one another".[20] Within such a context, teaching is what occurs when a student begins to understand what he or she is doing in connection with his or her experience and interpretation of reality, as well as what allows such students to recognize errors and to propose solutions.[21]

As David Denton explains in his essay "That Mode of Being Called Teaching," what this necessitates for schools is the development of curricula that will offer students at once a positive, fostering environment and an opportunity to develop the consciousness and the skills the will need to comprehend the various influences their culture exerts on their existence.[22] The next few pages provide concrete examples for educators of how to implement an existentialist curriculum within a classroom setting.

IMPLICATIONS FOR EDUCATORS: IMPLEMENTING A 'CURRICULUM OF ACTION' IN THE CLASSROOM

I. Implementing the concept of naming.

Students of education need to be made aware that the struggle over power relations and a struggle for meaning and interpretation must start with the individual being involved in the more rudimentary activity of naming. A related exercise I conduct in my classroom is entitled "Naming an Obstacle." My students have to articulate and name an obstacle they have been confronted with in their lives. The obstacle can be social, psychological, emotional, and/or physical. They are then required to explain how they overcame that obstacle, and in so doing, how they created a space where they embodied freedom. The emphasis in the exercise is to make the students realize the empowering effect of naming when confronted with an obstacle. Naming helps students to expose the oppression that they have been subjected to, and articulate methodologies to overcome that oppression. Encouraging our future teachers to explore the methods employed in creating their oppression and resulting pain, could help sensitize them to what oppression is, and how it occurs in the lives of their own students and in their institutions.

II. Connections between the private and the public.

Contextualizing a classroom based on Greene's pedagogy entails linking the language of the neighborhood, city, and state with the languages of other traditions: as Giroux says, "a postmodern curricula in which storytelling evokes memories shared and histories made through the affirmation of difference, struggle and hope. Suggesting that the curriculum be tailored to the voices that students already have, so they can extend those voices to other galaxies, is less familiar but equally important" (Giroux, 1988). Consequently, if the function of democracy in education is to communicate human experiences in terms of freedom, association, and liberty, then students and teachers can use creative pedagogical strategies to educate one another. An example of such an exercise is the "Pedagogical Narrative" that I use in my classroom: I instruct my students to write narratives based on their autobiographical experiences. The aim of this exercise is to make students reflect critically on their individual pedagogies.

The students' experiences narrated through their speaking and writing, voice the fears, struggles, and biases students bring into their learning space, and encourages them to continually deconstruct their own narratives that are often at the center of their own teaching. This exercise makes students aware that pedagogy becomes not only a matter of teaching—it embodies their experiences. Educators have to be in a process of examining and re-examining, creating and recreating themselves as teachers in relation to their students. The goal of this exercise is to transform a teacher's consciousness to a level where they can become critical and reflective practitioners. Questioning their own subjective ideologies will also make teachers aware of their social and subjective positions in the power structure and further question the relationship between pedagogy and identity, and the role of agency in their own classroom.

III. Creating decentered spaces.

What spaces do our students occupy when they are present in their class-rooms and what spaces do they occupy once they leave? All teachers can explore similar questions by engaging in activities that begin to deconstruct their student's narratives and inform public spaces in their own classrooms. An exercise I conduct in class with my students involves creating a lesson plan, with an emphasis on asking the students in my classes why they are implementing the methods they are advocating in their own classrooms. This exercise, called the "Epistemic Exercise," asks my students to engage in "deconstructing their epistemologies" by answering the following questions:

1) How do students in K–12 classrooms construct knowledge? (Why they have their belief system.)
2) How is that belief system assessed?
3) What kind of students does this model produce?

As a result of the "Epistemic Exercise" my students understand why they are so resistant to thinking outside a structural paradigm. Furthermore they comprehend the fact that to be effective and successful educators, they have to be engaged in continuously examining and re-examining their own belief system in keeping with the students they teach. As a result of this exercise, students begin to question power, examine socialized values, and understand the collaborative relationship between themselves and social change. The 'space' of a classroom becomes public when students learn from each other and respond as engaged participants as the learning environment values sharing, listening and reflection.

IV. Empowering students and creating a new language.

Teaching is both a public and a private activity, calling on both narrative and analytic ways of knowing. When students explore issues such as creating 'public spaces' through the construction of various perspectives and subjectivities, they begin to engage in rich classroom interactions where they express their feelings and ideas through oral and written mediums. Such engagements are grounded in encouraging students to come into consciousness of difference marked by various poetic and creative styles.

In my classroom, students are invited to work as a group on a project related to education; where they are given a chance to research and inform their peers about an issue of concern to them. Students are encouraged to incorporate alternative and innovative means of conveying their ideas to the class. This work implies a commitment on the part of students to engage alternate discourses and creative acts of reading, writing, and meaning, thus opening their own classroom spaces to include multiple situationalities. By integrating theater, creative arts, music, and literature in my courses, my students are then able to engage in the process of negotiation and translation around a 'third space' in which diversity and difference offer new possibilities for producing meanings, representations and democratic roles.

These suggested exercises motivate students of education to embrace the challenge of self-actualization as it manifests itself in their individual pedagogies and learning. The overarching goal in these exercises is to further expand a student's pedagogical perspective in light of Greene's pedagogy of action, consequently moving them to action by transforming their own classrooms.

By drawing on Greene's existential philosophy of education, I have proposed a method that would bring forward existential curriculum opportunities through which students could experience self-empowerment and freedom within a social framework. The pedagogy I offer in this book integrates student narratives, democratic schooling, and the social reconstruction of imagination into a curriculum of action, in which students have ownership over their subject matter. Such a curriculum provides students with actively engaging in the forces that determine how they construct knowledge. It is within this interpretation of education that individuals can be encouraged to interpret what they see and read and can begin to derive meaning from the world by which they are surrounded. The work that I have proposed is not something that can be easily carried to full fruition. It requires a continuing struggle to explore what democracy, dignity, and diversity mean, and to imagine ways of bringing them to life in the curriculum. I can only hope that the present work may provide an opening to this path.

*A revised version of this chapter can be found at Rasheed S., "Naming and the Existentialist Curriculum of Action: Creating a Pluralistic Pedagogy. ". *International Journal of Pedagogies and Learning*, 1(2), October 2005, an open access journal whose articles are free to use, with proper attribution, in educational and other non-commercial settings.

NOTES

1. For further discussion on this topic see "Maxine Greene and the Current/Future Democratization of Curriculum Studies," James Henderson, Janice Hutchion, and Charlene Newman, in William F. Pinar, ed., *The Passionate Mind of Maxine Greene: "I am . . . not Yet* (London: Falmer Press, 1998), 207.

2. Maxine Greene, *Releasing the Imagination: Essays on Education, the Arts, and Social Change* (San Francisco: Jossey-Bass Inc., 1995), 172.

3. Ibid. 170.

4. James Henderson, Janice Hutchion, and Charlene Newman, "Maxine Greene and the Current/Future Democratization of Curriculum Studies," 202.

5. Ibid., 206.

6. Jesse Goodman and Julie Teel, "The Passion of the Possible: Maxine Greene, Democratic Community, and Education," in William F. Pinar, ed., *The Passionate Mind of Maxine Greene: "I am . . . not Yet* (London: Falmer Press, 1998), 64

7. Greene, *Dialectic of Freedom,* (New York: Teachers College Press, 1988) 116

8. Greene, *Releasing the Imagination*, 163

9. Ibid., 163–4.

10. See Jesse Goodman and Julie Teel, "The Passion of the Possible: Maxine Greene, Democratic Community, and Education,"

11. Greene, "The Passions of Pluralism: Multiculturalism and the Expanding Community," *Educational Researcher*, 22 (1993), pp. 17–18

12. Greene, *The Dialectic of Freedom*, 126

13. Maxine Greene, "Reflection and Passion in Teaching," Journal of Curriculum and Supervision, (1986), 2(1), 74.

14. Greene, *Releasing the Imagination* 161

15. ibid., 1

16. Greene, *Landscapes of Learning* (New York: Teachers College Press, 1978), 61.

17. Greene, *Releasing the Imagination*, 172.

18. Greene, *Teacher as Strange: Educational Philosophy for the Modern Age*, (Belmont, Calif.: Wadsworth Publishing Company, 1973) 159.

19. Maxine Greene, "Values: Education in the Contemporary Moment," The Clearing House 64 (1991), 301–04.

20. Maxine Greene, "Values: Education in the Contemporary Moment," 122.

21. Greene, *Teacher as Stranger*, 172.

22. David E. Denton, "That Mode of Being Called Teaching," in David E. Denton (ed.) Existentialism and Phenomenology in Education: Collected Essays (New York: Teachers College Press, 1974), 115.

Bibliography

Anderson, Thomas C. *Sartre's Two Ethics: From Authenticity to Integral Humanity*. Illinois: Open Court Publishing Company, 1993.

———. *The Structure and Foundation of Sartrean Ethics*. Kansas: Regents Press, 1979.

Apple, Michael W. *Ideology and Curriculum*. New York: Routledge, 1979.

———. "Series Editor's Introduction." In *Capitalist Schools*, edited by D. Liston. New York: Routledge, 1988.

Arendt, Hannah. *The Human Condition*. Chicago: Chicago University Press, 1958.

Ayers, W. "Interview with Maxine Greene." *Qualitative Studies in Education* 8/4 (1995): 319–328.

Benhabiba, Khemais. "Sartre's Existentialism and Education: The Missing Foundation of Human Relations." *Educational Theory* 23/3 (Summer 1973). 230–239.

Brown, Robert K. "Max Manen and Pedagogical Human Science Research." In *Understanding Curriculum as Phenomenological and Deconstructed Text*, edited by William. F. Pinar and William M. Reynolds. New York: Teachers College Press, 1992. 44–63.

Cole, David. "Strategies of Difference: Litigating for Women's Rights in a Man's World." *Law and Inequality: Journal of Theory and Practice* 2 (February 1984): 45.

Connel, Robert Williams. "Poverty and Education." *Harvard Educational Review* 64/2 (Summer 1994): 125–149.

de Beauvoir, Simone. *Force of Circumstance*, trans. Richard Howard. New York: G.P. Putnam's Sons, 1964.

———. *The Second Sex*, translated and edited by H. M. Parshley. New York: Knopf, 1953.

Denton, David E. "That Mode of Being Called Teaching." In *Existentialism and Phenomenology in Education: Collected Essays*, edited by David E. Denton. New York: Teachers College Press 1974. 99–115.

Dewey, John. *On Experience, Nature and Freedom*, edited by Richard Bernstein. New York: The Liberal Arts Press, 1960.

Dillon, M.C. *Merleau-Ponty's Ontology*. Indianapolis: Indiana University Press, 1998.

Eagleton, Terry. *Literary Theory: An Introduction*. Minneapolis: University of Minnesota Press, 1983.

Freire, Paulo. *Pedagogy of the Oppressed*. Trans. Myra Bergman Ramos. New York: Continuum Publishing Company. 1999.

——. *Pedagogy of the Oppressed*. New York: Seabury Press, 1968.

Fruchter, Norm. "Pursuing Public Space: Maxine Greene and Sameness in Utter Diversity." In *A Light in Dark Time: Maxine Greene and the Unfinished Conversation*, edited by William Ayers and Janet L. Miller. New York: Teachers College Press, 1998. 229–240.

Garrison, James E. "Greene's Dialectics of Freedom and Dewey's Naturalistic Existential Metaphysics." *Educational Theory* 40/2 (Spring 1990): 193–209.

Giroux, Henry. *Border Crossings: Cultural Workers and the Politics of Education*. New York: Routledge, 1992.

——. *Living Dangerously: Multiculturalism and the Politics of Difference*. New York: Peter Lang Press, 1993.

Giroux, Henry A., Anthony N. Penna, and William F. Pinar. *Curriculum and Instruction in Education: Alternatives in Education*. California: McCutchen Publishing Corporation, 1981.

Greene, Maxine. "How Do We Think About Our Craft?" In *Rethinking School Improvement: Research, Craft and Concept*, edited by Ann Lieberman. New York: Teachers College Press, 1986. 13–25.

——. "Reflection and Passion in Teaching." *Journal of Curriculum and Supervision* 2/1: 68–81. 1986.

——. *Landscapes of Learning*. New York: Teachers College Press, 1978.

——. "Values Education in the Contemporary Moment." *The Clearing House* 64/3: 1–4. 1991.

——. *Dialectic of Freedom*. New York: Teachers College Press, 1988.

——. "Literature, Existentialism and Education." In *Existentialism and Phenomenology in Education: Collected Essays*, edited by David E. Denton. New York: Teachers College Press, 1974. 63–86.

——. "In Search of a Critical Pedagogy." In *The Transformative Power of Critical Pedagogy*, edited by Pepi Leistyna, Arlie Woodrum, and Stephen A. Sherblum. Cambridge, Mass.: Harvard Educational Review, 1996. 13–29.

——. *Teacher as Stranger: Educational Philosophy for the Modern Age*. Belmont, Calif.: Wadsworth Publishing Company, 1973.

——. *Releasing the Imagination: Essays on Education, Arts, and Social Change*. San Francisco: Jossey-Bass Publishers, 1995.

——. *Existential Encounters for Teachers*. New York: Random House, 1967.

——. *Education, Freedom and Possibility* (Inaugural Lecture as William F. Russell Professor). New York: Teachers College, Columbia University, 1975).

——. "Public Spaces in Local Places." *Phenomenology and Pedagogy* 10 (1992): 243–251.

_____. "Metaphors and Multiples: Representation, the Arts, and History." *Phi Delta Kappan* (January 1997). 387–394.

——. "Foreword." In *Inquiry and Reflection: Framing Narrative Practice in Education*, edited by Diane Dubose Brunner. Albany: State University of New York Press, 1994. I-xix.

——. "The Lived World." In *The Education Feminist Reader*, edited by Lynda Stone. New York: Routledge Press, 1994. 17–25.

——. "How I Came to Phenomenology." *Phenomenology and Pedagogy* 1 (1983): 3–4.

——. "The Passions of Pluralism: Multiculturalism and the Expanding Community." Educational Researcher 22, 1 (1993) 13–18.

Goodman, Jesse, and Julie Teel "The Passion of the Possible: Maxine Greene, Democratic Community, and Education" In *The Passionate Mind of Maxine Greene: "I am . . . not Yet*, edited by William F. Pinar. London: Falmer Press, 1998. 60–75.

Grumet, Madeline R. "Existential and Phenomenological Foundations of Autobiographical Methods." In *Understanding Curriculum as a Racial Text: Representations of Identity and Difference in Education*, edited by Louis A. Castenell, Jr. and William F. Pinar. Albany: State University of New York Press, 1993. 28–43.

——. *Bitter Milk: Women and Education*. Amherst: University of Massachusetts Press, 1988.

Hawthorne, Nathaniel. "The May-Pole of Merry Mount." In *Selected Tales and Sketches*. New York: Penguin Books, 1987. 138–149.

Helle, Anita Plath. "Reading Women's Autobiographies: A Map of Reconstructed Knowing." In *Stories Lives Tell: Narrative and Dialogue in Education*, edited by Nel Noddings and Carol Witherall. New York: Teachers College Press, 1991. 48–66.

Henderson, James, Janice Hutchion, and Charlene Newman. "Maxine Greene and the Current/Future Democratization of Curriculum Studies." In *The Passionate Mind of Maxine Greene: "I am . . . not Yet*, edited by William F. Pinar. London: Falmer Press, 1998. 190–212.

Jacobs, Mary-Ellen. "Living Dangerously: Towards a Poetics of Women's Lived Experience." In *A Light in Dark Time: Maxine Green and the Unfinished Conversation*, edited by William Ayers and Janet L. Miller. New York: Teachers College Press, 1988. 180–189.

Kohli, Wendy. "Philosopher of/for Freedom." In *A Light in Dark Times: Maxine Greene and the Unfinished Conversation*. New York: Teachers College Press, 1998. 11–21.

Luce-Kapler, Rebecca. "The Slow Fuse of Aesthetic Practice." In *The Passionate Mind of Maxine Greene: I am . . . not Yet*, edited by William F. Pinar. London: Falmer Press, 1998. 148–159.

——. *Philosophy and Education: Dimensions of Philosophy Series*. Boulder, Colo.: Westview Press, 1995.

McLaren, Peter L.. "Critical Pedagogy: Constructing an Arch of Social Dreaming and a Doorway to Hope." *Journal of Education* (1992). 77–100.

Merleau-Ponty, Maurice. *Phenomenology of Perception*. London: Routledge and Kegan Paul, 1967.

Morris, Marla. "Existential and Phenomenological Influences on Maxine Greene." In *The Passionate Mind of Maxine Greene: "I am . . . not Yet*, edited by William F. Pinar. London: Falmer Press, 1998. 124–136.

Morrison, Toni. *The Bluest Eye*. New York: Bantam Books, 1970.

Moyana, Toby Tafirenyika. *Education, Liberation and the Creative Act*. Harare, Zimbabwe: Zimbabwe Publishing House, 1988.

Nieto, Sonia. *Affirming Diversity: The Sociopolitical Context of Multicultural Education*, 2nd ed. New York: Longman, 1995.

Noddings, Nel. "Ethics and Imagination." In *A Light in Dark Time: Maxine Greene and the Unfinished Conversation*, edited by William Ayers and Janet L. Miller. New York: Teachers College Press, 1988. 159–169.

Olafson, Frederick A. "Authenticity and Obligation." In *Sartre: A Collection of Critical Essays*, edited by Mary Warnock. Garden City, N.Y.: Anchor Books, 1971. 121–175.

Pinar, William F. "Notes on the Curriculum Field" In *Autobiography, Politics and Sexuality: Essays in Curriculum Theory 1972–1992*. New York: Peter Lang Press, 1994. 77–100.

———. "Notes on Understanding Curriculum as a Racial Text." In *Race, Identity and Representation in Education*, edited by Cameron McCarthy and Warren Crichlow. London: Routledge Press, 1993.

Pinar, William F., and Louis A. Castenell, Jr. *Understanding Curriculum as Racial Text: Representations of Identity and Difference*. Albany: State University of New York Press, 1993.

Pinar, William F., and Madeline R. Grumet. *Toward a Poor Curriculum*. Dubuque, Iowa: Kendall Hunt Publishing Company, 1976.

Said, Edward W. *The World, the Text, the Critic*. Cambridge, Mass.: Harvard University Press 1983.

Sanchez, Ray. *John Dewey, Jean-Paul Sartre and the Modern Metaphysics of Value*. Ed. D Dissertation. Teachers College, Columbia University, 1961.

Sartre, Jean-Paul. *Being and Nothingness*, trans. Hazel E. Barnes. New York: Philosophical Library, 1956.

———. *Search for a Method*. New York: Alfred A. Knopf, 1963.

———. *The Transcendence of the Ego*, trans. Forest Williams. New York: Noonday, 1957.

———. *Psychology of Imagination*. New York: Philosophical Library, 1948.

———. *The Critique of Dialectical Reason*, trans. Alan. Sheridan-Smith. London: NLB, 1976.

———. *Existentialism and Human Emotion*, trans. Barnard Frechtman and Hazel Barnes. New York: Citadel Press, 1977.

———. *Saint Genet: Actor and Martyr*, trans. B. Frechtman. New York: New American Library, Mentor Books, 1963.

———. *Existentialism and Humanism*, trans. P. Mairet. London: Methuen Ltd., 1973.

———. *What is Literature?* New York: Philosophical Library, 1949.

Sizer, Theodore. *Horace's Compromise: The Dilemma of the American High School.* Boston: Houghton Mifflin, 1984.

Sleeter, Christine E., and P. McLaren, eds. *Multicultural Education, Critical Pedagogy and the Politics of Discourse.* Albany: State University of New York Press, 1995.

Tillich, Paul. *Courage to Be.* New Haven, Conn.: Yale University Press, 1952.

Trinh Minh-ha. *When the Moon Waxes Red.* New York: Routledge, 1991.

van Manen, Max. "The Utrecht School; An Experiment in Educational theorizing." *Interchange* 10/1, 48–66. 1979

———. "Edifying Theory; Serving the Good." *Theory into Practice* 21/1, 44–49. 1982

———. "Practical Phenomenological Writing." *Phenomenology and Pedagogy* 2/1. 36–39. 1984

———. "The Relation between Research and Pedagogy." In *Contemporary Curriculum Discourses*, edited by William F. Pinar. Scottsdale, Ariz.: Gorsuch Scarisbrick, 437–452. 1988.

———. *Researching Lived Experience; Human Science from an Action Sensitive Pedagogy.* London, Ontario: Althouse Press, 1988.

———. *The Tact of Teaching: The Meaning of Pedagogical Thoughtfulness.* Albany: State University of New York Press, 1991.

Warnock, Mary. *Existentialist Ethics.* London: MacMillan, 1967.

Young, Iris Marion. *Justice and the Politics of Difference.* Princeton, N.J.: Princeton University Press, 1990.